A PRACTICAL PLAN FOR DYNAMIC DEVOTIONS

GOD
alone
with

jason janz

JOURNEY
FORTH™

Greenville, South Carolina

Library of Congress Cataloging-in-Publication
Janz, Jason, 1973-
    Alone with God : a practical plan for dynamic devotions / Jason Janz.
        p. cm.
    Includes bibliographical references and index.
    ISBN 1-59166-625-2 (perfect bound pbk. : alk. paper)
    1. Christian life. I. Title.
    BV4501.3.J365 2006
    248.3—dc22

                                                    2006005302

The fact that materials produced by other publishers may be referred to in
this volume does not constitute an endorsement of the content or theological
position of materials produced by such publishers.

All Scripture is quoted from the Authorized King James version.

Alone with God: A Practical Plan for Dynamic Devotions

Design by Craig Oesterling
Composition by Melissa Matos

ISBN 1-59166-625-2

15 14 13 12 11 10 9 8 7 6 5 4 3 2 1

To my wife, Jennifer
Jonathan, I'm not. But Sarah, you are.

"*If you present all the world before her, with the richest of its treasures, she disregards it and cares not for it, and is unmindful of any pain or affliction. She has a strange sweetness in her mind and singular purity in her affections; is most just and conscientious in all her conduct; and you could not persuade her to do anything wrong or sinful, if you would give her all the world, lest she should offend this Great Being. She is of a wonderful sweetness, calmness and universal benevolence of mind; especially after this Great God has manifested himself to her mind. She will sometimes go about from place to place, singing sweetly; and seems to be always full of joy and pleasure; and no one knows for what. She loves to be alone, walking in the fields and groves, and seems to have some one invisible always conversing with her.*"

—*Jonathan Edwards on Sarah Pierrepont*
whom he eventually married

Table of Contents

1 It's All About a Relationship   1

2 The Foundation   9

3 The Need   18

4 The Myths   36

5 The Nuts and Bolts   54

6 The Covenant Friend   82

7 The Secret   93

8 The Life That Touches Lives   111

Appendix   115

Notes   149

Acknowledgements

To Suzette Jordan at the Press for believing in the project and Nancy Lohr, my editor, whose comments during the editing process were more of an encouragement than she will ever know.

To Joy McCarnan for her editing work. Her passion to use her gifts to support world-changing ministry is a challenge to all who know her.

To Joy Wagner for coming through in the clutch when I was avalanched by cyberspace during deadlines.

To Naomi Smoker for her tireless labor in preparing the manuscript for submission.

To Bob Roberts and Will Galkin. They are covenant friends who strengthen my hand in God.

To Steve Pettit for constantly bringing my focus back to what really matters. I know that when I'm in over my head, his cell phone number will show up on my caller ID.

To Les Ollila for exemplifying a life that was born out of a relationship with God. He still speaks to my soul.

To Pastor Heinze who has been my pastor for twenty years. His faithful shepherding has shaped my adult years more than anybody on the planet.

To Bart and Sandy Janz for implanting in me a desire to not just learn about God, but to know Him.

To Pete and Pat Darnell for living a life of close fellowship with the Lord that rubbed off in a colossal way on their daughter. I reap the benefits daily.

To my wife Jennifer for her tireless encouragement to "get it finished." Without her, the book would be another dream in fragment form.

To my boys. Every time I see them I am reminded that the depth of my relationship with God will have a life-shaping impact upon them.

To all the teens I worked with at Red Rocks. Their constant questions became the anvil upon which I endeavored to hammer out a simple plan to follow.

To the Red Rocks family. It has been an honor to serve them. "Doing life" together through His local church has been the most rewarding experience of my life.

1
it's all about a
Relationship

During my college years, I took a year off to travel. During that year, I took a trip that changed my life. My best friend and I planned a three-month missionary trip to Africa. We spent six weeks in the jungles of the Congo and six weeks in Kenya, a more modern African country. Plans developed smoothly until just before departure. I fell madly in love with a girl named Jennifer.

I knew that I wanted to marry her; I even knew when. I was going to propose on Christmas day of that year, about seven days after my return from Africa. Before I left, I told her for the first time that I loved her. My friend Will and I boarded a plane to go to a land about which we knew nothing. We landed in the center of the continent and headed up-stream. Our five-day journey was on a speedboat the missionary had just purchased. We took jungle trips by bicycle, Land Rover, and motorbike. What an experience! All I had to remind me of Jennifer was a gold-framed picture in my suitcase and memories. We left the Congo after six weeks of no contact with America. We flew to Nairobi, Kenya and went to the home of the missionary with whom we would be staying.

When I arrived in my living quarters, there on the pillow of my bed was a stack of letters from Jennifer. Wow! Nothing else mattered. I had not had a piece of chocolate in six weeks, and the missionary had loads of it. I didn't care; I wanted to read those letters. The letters had a soothing effect on my soul. Miraculously enough, the letters seemed to portray that she still loved me.

The missionary had hooked up his computer so that this new thing called an e-mail could be sent via computer to anyone else who had a computer with Internet access. I was able to find out Jen's address, and I sent her an e-mail. Sure enough, the next day, I received an e-mail from her. There was one problem. E-mail was in its infancy, and mine was garbled. Words were out of place and scrambled. Strings of letters that made no sense were between her real words. However, if I took my time, I could figure out what she was trying to say. It was like trying to decipher code. But you know what? It didn't matter. Words from her were what I wanted. The cryptic search actually made the experience more enjoyable.

I still have those letters, and they are some of the mile markers on the road of our relationship. All I wanted was a relationship with the girl I loved. Deciphering her letters wasn't a chore; it was a fruit of a good relationship. Now, after marriage, several children, and years of spending every day together, it's nice to look back and remember. As I read over those old e-mails, it is obvious to me how our relationship has matured over the years. The depth of communication then cannot be compared to the level enjoyed as a result of a healthy, ten-year marriage.

This is a book about a relationship: not a relationship with a friend or a lover or a co-worker but a relationship with God—the God of the universe. He created you to have a relationship with Him. Many times when individuals think about their deepest relationships, they think of a spouse or a best friend. In reality, they should think of God and feel closer to God than to any human. When individuals begin to develop a relationship, they want to spend time with those people to learn more about them and vice versa. The difference between that type of relationship and a relationship with God is that God already knows everything about your past, present, and future. The only one who needs to grow in the relationship is you. You need to learn everything you can about God—His past, present, and future workings. Learning more about God will be accomplished only by spending time with Him. Yet many believers seem to struggle through "deciphering the words" of the Bible because it seems difficult to understand. At first glance, God seems difficult to understand. We naturally run from things we do not understand.

John 15 explains that God desires to have you graduate in your relationship to Him to a higher level. Many believers see themselves as servants of God. However, according to John 15:15, there is a deeper, more meaningful relationship than being a servant. You can be God's friend. The Bible says the servant does not know what his master does, but Christ says you are His friend because He has made known to you everything that God has communicated to Him. God desires for you to graduate from simply a servant mentality to a friend mentality. This book is written to help you do that. The depth of your relationship with God is what is going to matter. When you are in love with someone, there will be times when you will struggle through understanding their words and you may feel distant from them; these should seem like small obstacles in comparison to your desire for a strong relationship.

The Status of the Relationship

George Barna, a Christian pollster, says that seven out of ten Americans (Christian and non-Christian) say that having a close, personal relationship with God is a top priority in their life.[1] However, all you have to do is look around, and you will see that the desires and the actions of the average American do not match. According to one survey, the average American prays less than five minutes a day, and the average Bible reader spends less than eight minutes a day in the Word of God[2]—hardly stuff to write home about. Worse yet, only eighteen percent of born-again Christians read the Bible every day and twenty-three percent never read the Bible at all.[3] So there is a major disconnect between what people want and what people do. What's new? The same condition exists in people's exercise programs, diet plans, career paths, and family time. The good news is that most believers don't want their relationship with God to be this way—stagnant. They are dissatisfied with their spiritual walk; they have a strong desire to make changes, but they are discouraged at their lack of success.

My "Aha" Moment

By the time I began college, I had grown weary of cold Christianity. I wanted more. I wanted to know God. Our Christian college president continually encouraged us to know God intimately, not just intellectually. Part of our college requirement was to spend thirty minutes a day with God before classes. For the first time in my life, I began to "taste and see that the Lord is good" (Psalm 34:8). Until that time, I had never truly had a taste of what a dynamic relationship with God could be like. I would like to say that because of this "forced habit" in college, I have not struggled keeping my daily quiet time with God since graduation. The reality is that consistency has been an issue since the day I left. I was just like the average believer—I wanted it, I had tasted it, but I wasn't following through.

My journey to finding a satisfying relationship with God took an unusual path. It happened as a result of "working out." Since graduation from college, I have married, started a family, and entered full-time ministry. My wife and I were content with many things in our life, but one area was constantly weak: physical fitness. We talked about working out consistently and had gone through different fits of bike riding and jogging; I even stooped so low as to try an aerobics video with my wife. But I gave it up when I tripped over my feet twice in one workout. My dream of having the lean, mean, muscle machine I had on my wedding day was over.

One day a good friend told me that I needed to change. He said, "Your body is running on your youth, but it won't last." I knew he was right. He had worked out for years and encouraged me to try a program called *Body for Life*. I thought, *Hey, I could at least buy the book and feel good that I investigated it.* However, when I finally got the book and read it, I was motivated. I gave the book to Jen and she experienced the same motivation. I bought a weight set to put in our garage. We already had a treadmill that was serving as a clothes hanger. I moved the treadmill into the garage and began to work out.

My wife and I began the program and within three weeks we were completely sold! I began to see that I did have muscles in my body. They were just "visually challenged." I'll never forget when I looked in the mirror and saw a line of indention running down the middle of my stomach! Unbelievable! I was well on my way to a coveted "six-pack abdomen." My clothes began to fit again, I woke up refreshed, and I just felt better about my body.

The author had written about one of the greatest needs in America today: physical fitness. As a pastor, I thought, *What is the greatest need of people today?* The answer rang loud and clear in my mind: spiritual fitness.

On the Road to Spiritual Fitness

Why is it that our culture is so concerned with the outside and not the inside? Why does the body get so much attention and not the soul? We are conditioned to pay so much attention to what people see and so little attention to what God sees. Clement of Alexandria, an early church father, said, "Those who adorn only the exterior, but neglect the inner man, are like the Egyptian temples, which present every kind of decoration upon the outside, but contain within, in place of a deity, a cat, a crocodile, or some other vile animal."[4] Could it be that we spend so little time with our God that our view of God is simply of a being who has only the power of a cat or crocodile?

The Bible says in Jeremiah 9:23–24, "Let not the wise man glory in his wisdom, neither let the mighty man glory in his might, let not the rich man glory in his riches: But let him that glorieth glory in this, that he understandeth and knoweth me." A higher goal than physical fitness or earthly wealth is to know God. My mind began to churn as my experiences in college and my most recent experiences began to meld. How could I make spiritual fitness a priority in my life? Could a plan be developed that would facilitate the development of a transforming relationship with God?

I needed a plan to get me going. The methods I had used before left me frustrated, bored, and eventually in despair. Every New Year, I resolved to get up earlier to spend more quality time with God. I had purchased the Bible memory packets that were supposed to revolutionize my memory habits. I had experimented with various Bible reading plans. I even tried to salve my conscience by listening to Christian radio or tapes on the way to work if I slept too late. The truth of the matter is that I was in as bad shape spiritually as I was physically.

I was motivated beyond thinking about it. I felt I needed a Bible-based approach centered on developing a relationship with God. I began to experiment with a plan for myself. I went back to look at how I had planned my workout every day and incorporated some of the same concepts into my personal "spiritual fitness plan." Wow! What a difference! I began to experience a regular, fulfilling, refreshing time with God. Over the next months, I began to share my thoughts with close friends and family. I mentioned it when I taught classes to high school and college students. Without exception, people asked me for more details on the plan. I began to see that the hunger for a tangible devotional plan was immense.

The Hunger for a Relationship

Over the last several years, I have come to believe the average American believer does not lack the desire for a stronger relationship with God but does lack the motivation, the know-how, and the structure to help along the way. We know believers who seem to have tremendous walks with God: we desire it and thirst for it. J. Oswald Sanders says, "It is an incontrovertible fact that some Christians seem to experience a much closer intimacy with God than others. They appear to enjoy a reverent familiarity with Him that is foreign to us."[5] For example:

Enoch walked with God so intensely that God did not let him see death; He took him straight to heaven (Genesis 5:24).

Abraham was called the friend of God (James 2:23).

Christ recognized Mary as having her relationship with God as her spiritual priority (Luke 10:42).

Moses was so close to God that God spoke to him face to face as a man speaks to his friend (Exodus 33:11).

David was known as a man after God's own heart (1 Samuel 13:14).

John was the disciple whom Jesus loved (John 21:7).

I have yet to meet a Spirit-filled believer who would not love to have this type of relationship with the God of the universe. Yet we should not look at these believers with a dreamy-eyed I-could-never-do-that mentality. Every believer has the same capacity as these Bible heroes to know our great God.

What's Out There?

I went to the local Christian bookstore to peruse resources available to help individuals develop this relationship. On one end, I found books written about the philosophy of Christian growth, how to study the Bible, the pattern of discipleship, the need for a passionate walk with God, and the need for a God-centered life. These books seemed to be strong on philosophy but short on practicality.

On the other end, I found daily devotionals that endeavored to make the Bible simple to understand. However, these devotionals not only interpreted and applied the Bible passage but also left the individual with no need to open the Bible. I also noticed that prayer was missing as an integral part of these plans. Often only a short written prayer was included at the bottom of the devotional for the reader to recite.

My greatest concern about these plans was the lack of an emphasis on biblical meditation and the character of God. It seemed there was more meditation on a short illustration or a cute story than on the passage of Scripture. The trend seemed to be letting gifted authors think for you. Their efforts were well intentioned—to help people walk with God daily. However, something was missing.

My desire was to bridge the gap between philosophy and practicality. I wanted to create something grounded in truth yet as practical as a recipe for making macaroni and cheese. Lest I am misunderstood, I have not tried to create a "formula approach" to the Christian life or tried to provide the "missing link" to all spiritual problems—this is not a happy pill. I see this book as a key to helping individuals unlock the door to a room full of the vast riches of a dynamic relationship with God. My goal is to make it simple for believers who hunger for God to take steps to become a stronger and more mature believer. One could say this is a manual designed to help you fall in love with God.

The core heartbeat of this book is to motivate you to deepen your relationship with God. The method is an eight-step self-guided process that gives you tools to worship God in a personal way.

The Results

A good spiritual fitness program will have extraordinary results. The Bible promises that those who spend time getting to know God will be strong and take action (Daniel 11:32). Hearing the stories of those who have entered this type of satisfying relationship has filled my heart with great joy. I trust that your journey will be worthwhile and fulfilling and that you will experience a relationship with the God of the universe unlike anything you've ever known.

This book was not borne out of my success but out of my failure. If you are like me, when you think about your walk with God, you sometimes feel weak, guilty, and discouraged. I want to encourage you to draw closer to God by spending greater amounts of time with Him. It is not rocket science. Before long you will grow in grace and begin to look like Him.

Coming Up

In the following chapters, you will find the big picture of spiritual growth. What do you want to become? You will look into the needs of a life-long relationship with God. One chapter deals with commonly held myths about quiet time. The "Nuts and Bolts" chapter maps out the eight-step method that is the foundation of a blossoming relationship with God. An explanation of biblical meditation gives you the ability to concentrate on God's character all day long. One of the final chapters discusses true friendships, and shows how they help you develop your relationship with God.

2
the
Foundation

The Perfect Relationship

In the beginning, it was perfect. Man's relationship with God was the best it has ever been. When God created man in His image, He stamped us with uniqueness. I believe part of the image of God in man is man's capacity to commune with God. We are spiritual people capable of fellowship with God. James Boice says, "Man is made for communion with God, who is Spirit. . . . This communion is intended to be eternal as God is eternal. . . . It is on the level of the spirit that he is aware of God and communes with Him."[1] This was the perfect condition of God's creation—unbroken fellowship and communion with the Creator of the universe.

The Relationship Broken

Sin put a breach in that communion with God. In Genesis 3, the story is told of how Satan lied about God to Eve. Caving in to their desires, Adam and Eve ate of the forbidden fruit and plunged the world into darkness. God came walking in the garden and summoned them to give an account for their actions. "Where art thou?" Before long, judgment had been pronounced and a curse instated. Mankind died that day, both physically and spiritually.

As a result of Adam's sin, every child ever born was born in sin. Romans 5:12 says, "Wherefore, as by one man sin entered into the world, and death by sin; and so death passed upon all men, for that all have sinned." We were all born without a relationship with our Creator.

In an unredeemed state, men and women cannot enjoy a relationship with God. The Bible clarifies that nobody naturally seeks after God. Unless our sin is removed, there is no hope for a restoration of that communion Adam and Eve knew with God in the garden.

The Relationship Restored

God did not leave us entirely without hope. In fact, even while God pronounced the curse upon humanity, He gave the first glimmer of the gospel, the only hope for that kind of restoration. In the form of a curse on Satan, Genesis 3:15 became the first prophecy of the Messiah to come. "And I will put enmity between thee and the woman, and between thy seed and her seed; it shall bruise thy head, and thou shalt bruise his heel." I can imagine Adam and Eve lifting up their heads as they heard that gospel for the first time. Satan would bruise the heel of Christ on the cross, but Christ would deliver the final, crushing blow of defeat upon Satan's head.

In due time Jesus Christ did come. He was called the second Adam. Just as Adam plunged all of humanity with him into sin, Jesus Christ provided salvation for all those who trust in His righteousness. Romans 5:17–19 says, "For if by one man's offence death reigned by one; much more they which receive abundance of grace and of the gift of righteousness shall reign in life by one, Jesus Christ. Therefore as by the offence of one judgment came upon all men to condemnation; even so by the righteousness of one the free gift came upon all men unto justification of life. For as by one man's disobedience many were made sinners, so by the obedience of one shall many be made righteous."

How can a human being make peace with God? Only by the grace of God. We can be justified from all sin by the work of Christ alone.

This justifying work of Christ is a gift to us, received by faith—a gift we cannot earn by our own works. When we are justified, God declares that He has accepted the substitutionary death of Christ on the cross as a payment for our debts, and the righteousness of Jesus Christ is imputed to us.

Perhaps you are wondering, "How do I receive this gift?" You must respond to the call of the gospel. Every person must repent of his sins and place his trust in Christ alone for salvation. Repentance is a heartfelt sorrow for sin, a renouncing of it, and a sincere commitment to forsake it and walk in obedience to Christ. Saving faith is trust in Jesus Christ as a living person for forgiveness of sins and eternal life with God.[2] When you repent and believe the gospel, you are adopted into God's family. The relationship is restored, and you can have communion with God.

Upon salvation, God places within the believer a hunger for Him. Philippians 2:13 says, "For it is God which worketh in you both to will and to do of his good pleasure." God works in every believer to help create the desire or will to do what God wants him to do, but the *desire* begins with God. This does not necessarily mean that at 6:00 a.m. when the alarm goes off, every believer automatically jumps out of bed, excited to open the Bible. However, it does mean that God has planted the desire and the ability within believers to have a close relationship with Him. David says in Psalm 42:1, "As the hart panteth after the waterbrooks, so panteth my soul after thee, O God. My soul thirsteth for God, for the living God." Deep within the heart of every believer is a longing for a close relationship with God. Psalm 73:25 says, "There is none upon earth that I desire beside thee." John Piper says, "In the end, the heart longs not for any of God's gifts, but for God Himself. To see Him and know Him and be in His presence is the soul's final feast."[3] This book is all about trying to help you experience a daily feast in the presence of God.

Getting Our Terms Right

From now on, when I talk about a relationship with God, I am not referring to the salvation of an individual. Once that initial bond is formed, it cannot be undone. When I am using the phrase "relationship with God," I will be referring to the communion between God and a believer. A synonymous phrase would be "walk with the Lord."

This book is designed to provide you with a simple, functional method for a daily private time with the Lord for prayer and Bible reading. I will use several terms interchangeably to describe this time, such as "quiet time," "daily walk," "devotions," or "time with God."

Key Contributors to a Growing Relationship with God

The Holy Spirit

The agent of change in the life of the believer is the Holy Spirit of God. The Holy Spirit resides in the believer and becomes a Guide, an Illuminator of biblical truth, and a Comforter. 2 Corinthians 3:18 says that we are changed into the image of Jesus Christ by the Holy Spirit. He is there "working under the hood," doing the actual work of change.

The Word of God

The means whereby a person learns more about God is the Bible. If you are going to have a devotional life of substance and strength, you must build it upon the Word of God.

The Bible is sufficient. You must come to the place where you believe the Bible when it says in 2 Peter 1:3, "According as his divine power hath given unto us all things that pertain unto life and godliness." *All things.*

The Bible is understandable. Psalm 119:105 says that the Word of God is "a lamp unto my feet, and a light unto my path." Lights are not confusing. They help repel the darkness. Although you may never understand every part of Scripture, God designed it so that it could be understood.

The Bible is also practical. The Bible talks about suffering, health, wisdom, worry, discipline, people skills, anger management, conquering sin habits, and more. It presents our world and human nature exactly as they are. The Bible truly is more relevant to your life than the daily newspaper.

Prayer and Bible Meditation

The practice of nurturing an authentic relationship with God will include prayer and meditation on God's Word. I prefer to describe this as a conversation with the Lord. A man who mastered this was George Mueller. He was born in Germany in 1805 and spent most of his life in Bristol, England. He was the most famous orphanage founder in history. During his lifetime, he cared for over ten thousand orphans, built five orphanages, and pastored the same church for sixty-six years. He also knew hardship. After enduring the agony of losing three children in infancy, he lost one wife after thirty-nine years of marriage and a second after twenty-three years of marriage. His faith in God was unusual as he never took on a debt, asked someone for money, or took a salary.

How did he do so much for God? He knew his God. He had a relationship with God. However, his daily walk was not without its frustrations. He shows us a window into a breakthrough in his own soul. In his biography of Mueller, A. T. Pierson includes an appendix called "Soul Nourishment First." This essay by Mueller explains how he went from dry times of personal prayer to a vibrant communion with God. (see appendix, pp. 145–148).

First Mueller describes how he changed his method to have his Bible reading first and his prayer second.

> *Before this time my practice had been, at least for ten years previously, as a habitual thing, to give myself to prayer, after having dressed in the morning. Now I saw, that the most important thing I was to do was give myself to the reading of the Word of God and to meditation on it, that thus my heart might be comforted, encouraged, warned, reproved, instructed; and thus, whilst meditating, my heart might be brought into experimental communion with the Lord.*[4]

Mueller describes the benefits of initially letting the Word of God work on his heart. Before long he was praying in the middle of his Bible reading.

> *The first thing I did, after having asked in a few words the Lord's blessing upon His precious Word, was to begin to meditate on the Word of God; searching, as it were, into every verse, to get blessing out of it . . . The result I have found to be almost invariably this, that after a very few minutes my*

soul has been led to confession, or to thanksgiving, or to intercession, or to supplication; so that though I did not, as it were, give myself to prayer, but to meditation, yet it turned almost immediately more or less into prayer.[5]

Mueller experienced fresh communion with God, and it had a direct impact on his day.

The result of this is . . . by breakfast time, with rare exceptions, I am in a peaceful and happy state of heart.[6]

He describes the difference this change of method wrought on his walk with God.

Formerly, when I rose, I began to pray as soon as possible, and generally spent all of my time till breakfast in prayer . . . But what was the result? I often spent a quarter of an hour, or half an hour, or even an hour on my knees before being conscious to my self of having derived comfort, encouragement, humbling of soul, etc.; and often after having suffered much from wandering of mind for the first ten minutes or quarter of an hour, I only then began to really pray.

I scarcely ever suffer now in this way. For my heart being nourished by the truth, being brought into experimental fellowship with God, I speak to my Father, and to my Friend (vile though I am, and unworthy of it!) about the things that He has brought before me in His precious Word."[7]

My desire in *Alone with God* is to help you experience the same refreshing friendship that Mueller experienced.

Seeing your devotional time as an opportunity to have a conversation with the Lord will help in developing a warm, intimate relationship with the Lord. When you read the Bible, you have one of two mindsets: a fact-based approach or a devotional, personal approach. The fact-based approach says, "What can I learn about the Bible today? Give me the facts." The personal approach says, "What is God saying to me today? What can I learn about the person and work of Christ? What affections need to be warmed in my heart?"

Just learning Bible facts will fill the mind, but when God becomes real, your heart will be full. The personal approach involves seeing the Bible as God's words to you and seeing prayer as your words to God. This results in a two-way conversation with God, pouring out your innermost heart to Him by worshipping Him passionately with your words, thoughts, and songs. At the same time, God is speaking to you, guiding you, and stirring your affections to a greater love for Him.

The Goal of a Growing Relationship with God

J. Oswald Sanders said, "One who loves with the emotions only will be a sentimentalist. One who loves with the will only will be a legalist. And one who loves with the intellect only will have little warmth. God desires the love of the whole personality."[8] But, how can you love God with your whole personality? Nobody speaks better on the issue of the development of the soul than Jonathan Edwards. In his book, *Religious Affections*, he thoroughly describes the function of the immaterial part of man. I will attempt to abridge his thoughts, but, realizing that my attempt will be inadequate at best, I recommend that you read this book in its entirety.

Edwards describes the affections as "vigorous and sensible exercises" of the soul. In other words, affections are not just mere exercises of the mind and the will, they are intense inclinations. Worship often can involve the mind, but if it doesn't stir up intense inclinations and desires for righteousness, it is dead.

One can exhibit positive or negative affections. Some examples of positive affections would be love, desire, hope, joy, gratitude, and contentment. Some examples of negative affections would be hatred, fear, anger, and grief. Some affections are the mixture of the two responses. For example, the affection of pity motivates the soul toward the person suffering as well as away from the suffering. Now when these inclinations are strong, you have an affection, and when they are sourced correctly and biblically, they are religious affections.

We tend to lump all of this talk into a category called the emotions. Yet Edwards would say it is far more complex than that. Edwards distinguishes two categories of what we call emotions: passions and affections. Passion is cheap emotion. It is sudden and can have a radical effect on the body. Affection is a strong action of the will or inclination. It is much deeper than mere passion. A passion is crying during a sad movie. An affection is found when one acknowledges his sinfulness, grieves over his fallenness, and confesses his sin to God. Godly affections are to be cultivated; passions are to be controlled. Passions are temporary, but affections endure.

Edwards says that the affections are the mainspring of human actions. By nature we are docile beings unless we are motivated by affections. The entire world works this way, for better or for worse. On the negative side, "Affection, indeed, is the motivation of the covetous man, the man who is greedy in worldly pursuits. They activate the lustful man in his pursuit of pleasure and sensual delights."[9] On the positive side, religious affections should cause the believer to pursue love, holiness, hope, joy, and mercy.

True religion should stimulate true, godly affection. The cultivation of godly affections should be the goal of every believer. This affection will manifest itself in a fear of the Lord, a hope in God, a hatred of sin, a hunger and thirst after righteousness, a godly sorrow, a holy joy, gratitude, and zeal for God. Too many believers seem to go through their Christian lives with little zeal for the things of God. Edwards' diagnosis would probably be that these Christians have not cultivated godly affections. "When the true beauty and attraction of the holiness found in divine things is discovered by the soul, a new world of perspectives is opened. The glory of all the perfections of God and of everything that pertains to Him is revealed."[10]

A good place to begin cultivating proper religious affections is in the Word of God. You must see God accurately, as He revealed Himself in His Word, in all of His glory and beauty. When you spend time in the Word of God, you want His Word to blow on the flame of your heart to change you to be more like Him. When you see God for who He is, desires for godliness are stirred up. These affections are more than just an intellectual understanding of facts about God, they are experiential. John Piper, an avid Edwards enthusiast, sums it up this way, "Worship must have heart and head. Worship must engage emotions and thought. Truth without emotion produces dead orthodoxy and a church full . . . of artificial admirers (like people who write generic anniversary cards for a living). On the other hand, emotions without truth produce empty frenzy and cultivate shallow people who refuse the discipline of rigorous thought. But true worship comes from people who are deeply emotional who also love deep and sound doctrine. Strong affections for God rooted in truth are the bone and marrow of biblical worship."[11]

When godly affections are cultivated, they will result in fervent worship. Piper goes on to say that worship services have become dead because "for many, Christianity has become the grinding out of general doctrinal laws from collections of biblical facts. But childlike wonder and awe have died. The scenery and poetry and music of the majesty of God have dried up like a forgotten peach at the back of the refrigerator."[12] The cultivation of godly affections will turn stale devotions into fervent personal worship of our holy God.

Your Personal Relationship

If you have not yet established an essential relationship with the Lord through conversion, I want to encourage you to do so before continuing in the book. You can read more about conversion on pages 143–144 of the appendix.

If you have been saved, the Holy Spirit is indwelling you, ready and willing to reveal the things of God to you. I trust that you will begin to take seriously the quest for a growing walk with God.

3
the
Need

Imagine preparing your home for the arrival of Christ and His followers, for whom you are also preparing a meal. However, this would be no small dinner party. Some commentators say that Christ traveled with as many as one hundred and fifty people, but even if it were only He and the disciples, to have the Son of God over for dinner would send chills down the spine of any hostess. The home Christ chose was none other than that of Mary and Martha, sisters to Lazarus. As the party was waiting for dinner to be served, Christ was in the living area, teaching. Mary, not wanting to miss what the Master had to say, sat at His feet and hung on His every word. Meanwhile, Martha was busy cooking the meal.

You can imagine the frustration Martha must have felt as she listened to everyone in the next room while she was doing the hard work, the important stuff. Her thoughts, particularly those about Mary, were probably less than edifying. Vindictive, maybe. Edifying, probably not. Martha was no different than you or I. The vegetables were not the only things steaming in the kitchen. Martha was mad. I can see her now. She grabs a towel, wipes her hands, wipes the sweat from her brow, straightens her apron, and marches into the living room. Walking up to Christ, she indignantly demands His help: "Master, don't you care that Mary has left me to serve the meal by myself? Tell her to help me."

Maybe Mary drops her head. Christ lifts up His eyes to Martha, and, with a few simple words, He puts time with God and service for God in their proper order for the rest of time and eternity: "Martha, Martha, thou art careful and troubled about many things: But one thing is needful: and Mary hath chosen that good part, which shall not be taken away from her." What a rebuke! Martha probably thought, perhaps a bit self-righteously, that Christ would identify with her point of view and correct the problem immediately. However, He did exactly the opposite. He said, in essence, that Mary was doing the right thing, listening to Him. He spoke right to Martha's heart. Not only did He address her current problem, He addressed her overall nature; she was careful and troubled about many things . . . except Him.

It doesn't seem like Martha ever changed. Less than a week before Jesus was to go to the Passover, He visited the home again. The Bible says "they made him a supper; and Martha served: but Lazarus was one of them that sat at the table with him. Then took Mary a pound of ointment of spikenard, very costly, and anointed the feet of Jesus, and wiped his feet with her hair: and the house was filled with the odour of the ointment."

The story in Luke 10 has probably played itself out in nearly every church and home. It is easy for believers to buy into Martha's philosophy that service for God—church attendance, weekly service, giving, witnessing—is as important as a walk with God. Actually, Christ says it is just the opposite—our walk with God takes a higher priority than our service for Him. A vibrant walk with God must be the priority in the lives of believers or they will find themselves tired, empty, and burnt out. I have been in the ministry long enough to see hundreds of people who once were the busiest servants in the church now sitting in weekly services with stone-cold looks on their faces. They were infected with the Martha virus, and they were never cured.

The greatest commandment in Scripture is to love the Lord your God with all your heart, soul, and mind (Matthew 22:37). When believers begin to make this relationship their priority, growth will take place.

These believers will have contagious joy, an abundant ministry, and a meaningful life. However, when believers are struggling, the first thing to check on is the consistency of their time with God. If people will turn to the Word of God and pursue a relationship with Him, they will find a cure for their many spiritual maladies.

Before believers can begin having an effective quiet time, they need to understand their needs. The plentiful resources available to believers today—conferences, seminars, books, and magazines—present conflicting messages that result in convoluted minds. My desire is to clarify the true needs of believers as they pertain to their daily devotions. Perhaps you will better understand the cause of your struggles when you get a true grasp of your needs.

The Need for Inner Renewal

As I stated in a previous chapter, Clement of Alexandria said, "Those who adorn only the exterior, but neglect the inner man, are like the Egyptian temples, which present every kind of decoration upon the outside, but contain within, in place of a deity, a cat, a crocodile, or some other vile animal."[1] Our tendency is to place emphasis on external adornment when God places the emphasis on internal change. 2 Corinthians 4:16b says, "Though our outward man perish, yet the inward man is renewed day by day." From the moment of birth, we began to die physically; however, our inner man can be renewed every day. So a seventy-year-old man can have the spirit of a teen boy!

Believers have sometimes placed the emphasis in the wrong area. As a result, outward conformity to certain standards of behavior has been equated with inner conformity to the will and ways of God. Rules have been handed down to help someone order his life; however, obedience to rules cannot be a valid sign that the heart is right with God. Believe me, I am not dismissing rules of conduct. I am personally a very conservative Christian. I believe that the grace of God teaches us that "denying ungodliness and worldly lusts, we should live soberly, righteously, and godly, in this present world" (Titus 2:12). I have seen, however, the negative results that come with an emphasis of rules over a relationship. The result is usually rebellion. God's purpose for His children is not external imitation, but internal transformation.

The crux of a Christian's growth is the inner renewal of the mind. Romans 12:2 says, "And be not conformed to this world: but be ye transformed by the renewing of your mind." *Renew* means "the adjustment of the moral and spiritual vision and thinking to the mind of God, which is designed to have a transforming effect upon the life."[2] This is where true change happens. Jim Berg says in his book *Changed into His Image*, "Having a renewed mind is not just memorizing a few Bible verses about a problem you are having, although that may be a start. It is not just becoming familiar with Christian principles and convictions about godly lifestyles. Having a renewed mind involves a relationship with your Creator that actually changes you because of your exposure to Deity."[3]

The Need to Seek God

The path to blessing in the Christian life is a fervent seeking after God. Hebrews 11:6 says that God is a "rewarder of them that diligently seek him." To *seek* means to search carefully. The same word that is used in Hebrews 11 for "seek" is used in 1 Peter 1:10, where we read that the Old Testament prophets searched their own inspired writings to learn about the salvation that was to come through Jesus Christ. Even though many of them actually wrote down the very words of the Scriptures, they searched them to learn as much as they could of the wonderful grace that was to come. They wanted to know everything they could about this coming suffering Messiah.

Seeking God, though, is not the end. Finding Him is. The Bible promises that if we seek Him, we will find Him. Jeremiah 29:13 says, "And ye shall seek me, and find me, when ye shall search for me with all your heart." Believers who seek after God will know God. J. I. Packer says in his book *Knowing God* that those who know God exhibit four qualities:

- *They have great energy for God – Daniel 11:32*
- *They have great thoughts of God – Daniel 2:20*

- *They show great boldness for God – Acts 20:24*

- *They have great contentment in God – Romans 5:1*[4]

But we cannot seek after God with all of our hearts while we are seeking fulfillment elsewhere. The Bible is explicit that man cannot serve two masters (Matthew 6:24). Seeking happiness through material possessions, earthly pleasures, popularity, and fame will only distance us from God. Jim Berg says, "Apathy toward God is the result of being passionate toward something or someone else."[5] If you feel distant from God, chances are you are seeking other things instead of Him. Decide today to seek Him with your whole heart. Lamentations 3:25 says, "The Lord is good unto them that wait for him, to the soul that seeketh him."

The Need for Dependence

George Barna found that ninety-two percent of Americans consider themselves self-sufficient.[6] It is not a far jump from self-sufficiency to self-dependence. In America we prize independence; however, we should never allow our independence to carry over into our spiritual life. Trust in God should be woven into the entire fabric of the Christian life, even though this is not often the case in our society. Our God-dependence has lessened over time while our self-dependence has grown. The Bible is quite clear that our dependence should not rest in ourselves, but upon God. Proverbs 3:5–6 instructs us to trust in the Lord with all our hearts and not to lean on our own understanding. Trust is truly God-dependence. Samuel Rutherford was a Scottish theologian who faced a life of extreme difficulty. He constantly faced persecution for his beliefs. However, he learned to depend on God even though he did not know what the future would hold. He left much in print, but perhaps he revealed his heart best when he said, "My faith hath no bed to sleep upon but Omnipotency."[7] In spite of trials, he anchored his life to Jesus Christ.

Any believer can become self-dependent; however, a daily quiet time with God will help us to keep the right perspective. One of the great influencers in my life was my college president, Dr. Les Ollila. He said over and over again in our chapel meetings, "Your time with God is not a declaration of your devotion, but a declaration of your dependence."

Come to God in daily Bible reading and prayer and cry out: "I need you, God."

The Need for Satisfaction in God

"Our Lord finds our desires, not too strong, but too weak. We are half-hearted creatures, fooling about with drink and sex and ambition when infinite joy is offered us, like an ignorant child who wants to go on making mud pies in a slum because he cannot imagine what is meant by the offer of a holiday at the sea. We are far too easily pleased."[8] This observation from C. S. Lewis shows how our materialistic society seeks alternative pleasures and chafes against finding true satisfaction in God. In fact, the devil constantly lures us into false contentment by promising the next thrill. Yet we as believers must become convinced that in Christ alone is true contentment. Christ not only promised life, He promised life more abundantly than anyone else could offer (John 10:10). He promised the best life. True satisfaction must come from a relationship with God. Our needs are met in Him; our joy flows from Him. John Piper said, "The greatest hindrance to worship is not that we are a pleasure-seeking people, but that we are willing to settle for such pitiful pleasures."[9] A devoted time with God every day will help cultivate a satisfaction in God.

I have included a Puritan prayer titled "Fullness" that illustrates this point in a heart-felt cry unto God. I would invite you to pray this prayer unto the Lord.

Heavenly Father,

Thou hast revealed to me myself as a mass of sin,
    And thyself as the fullness of goodness,
    With strength enough to succor me,
    Wisdom enough to guide me,
    Mercy enough to quicken me,
    Love enough to satisfy me.

Thou hast shown me that because thou art mine
    I can live by thy life,
    Be strong in thy strength,
    Be guided by thy wisdom;
    And so I can pitch my thoughts and heart in thee.

This is the exchange of wonderful love—
    for me to have thee for myself,
    and for thee to have me, and to give me thyself.

There is in thee all fullness of the good I need,
    And the fullness of all grace to draw me to thyself,
    Who else could never have come.

But having come, I must cleave to thee,
    Be knit to thee,
    Always seek thee.

There is none all good as thou art:
    With thee I can live without other things,
    For thou art God all-sufficient,
    And the glory, peace, rest, joy of the world
    Is a creaturely, perishing thing in comparison with thee.

Help me to know that he who hopes for nothing but thee,
    And for all things only for thee, hopes truly,
    And that I must place all my happiness in holiness,
    If I hope to be filled with all grace.

Convince me that I can have no peace at death,
    Nor hope that I should go to Christ,
    Unless I intend to do his will
    And have his fullness while I live.[10]

The Need for the Work of the Holy Spirit

The Holy Spirit indwells every believer. Christ walked this earth until the time came for Him to go to the cross and make the greatest sacrifice for the sins of humanity. His departure caused great distress among the disciples. However, Christ promised He would not leave them alone. He would send another Comforter, the Holy Spirit. You can imagine the fear the disciples felt as their leader declared His coming departure. However, this exchange was a better arrangement for the disciples—even though they did not realize it at the time. Whereas they felt sorry to lose Christ's tangible presence, they would soon realize they were exchanging it for the indwelling omnipresence of the Holy Spirit. The same is true for believers today. At salvation, the Holy Spirit of God comes to live inside a believer, to minister and rule in that believer's heart.

One of the Holy Spirit's ministries to the believer is to illuminate Bible truth. 1 Corinthians 2:6–16 gives us an in-depth look at the teaching ministry of the Holy Spirit in the life of the believer. Verses 12 and 13 say, "Now we have received, not the spirit of the world, but the spirit which is of God; that we might know the things that are freely given to us of God. Which things also we speak, not in the words which man's wisdom teacheth, but which the Holy Ghost teacheth; comparing spiritual things with spiritual." He teaches us the things of God and gives us the wisdom and the ability to apply and judge all things. Jonathan Edwards explained this in a sermon he preached, titled "A Divine and Supernatural Light, Immediately Imparted to the Soul by the Spirit of God, Shown to Be Both a Scriptural and Rational Doctrine." Edwards explains this light. "It may be thus described: A true sense of the divine excellency of the things revealed in the Word of God, and a conviction of the truth and reality of them thence arising." He is careful to warn that this new light "reveals no new doctrine, it suggests no new propositions to the mind, it teaches no new thing of God, or Christ or another world not taught in the Bible, but only gives a due apprehension of those things that are taught in the Word of God."[11]

We should be aware of the Holy Spirit's ministry of illumination every time we open the Word of God. David said in Psalm 119:18, "Open thou mine eyes, that I may behold wondrous things out of thy law." Before you begin reading your Bible, ask the Holy Spirit to be active in showing Christ to you. He will glorify the face of Jesus Christ to you. The result of this illuminating ministry of the Holy Spirit in our lives will be that we gain the mind of Christ. That's a wonderful thought.

The Need for a Word-Based Approach

Many believers are not having a satisfying quiet time because they are not Word-based, but merely devotional-based. Let me explain. Christian bookstores are full of daily devotionals designed to help individuals develop a closer walk with God. I am not against daily devotionals. I have used them in the past, and I appreciate those who put them together. I am concerned, however, that more and more people are relying upon the next new devotional to help them in their walk while neglecting to study the Bible.

It is almost as though some people think the Bible needs help, or at least that they require some help to read it. Perhaps people feel inadequate to understand the meaning on their own, and thus they feel more comfortable if a famous author explains it to them. The average amount of time that the majority of believers spend reading God's Word indicates how irrelevant people believe the Bible to be.

David's description of the Word of God must seem strange to many believers. Here are just some excerpts from Psalm 119.

Psalm 119:14—*I have rejoiced in the way of thy testimonies, as much as in all riches.*

Psalm 119:16—*I will delight myself in thy statutes: I will not forget thy word.*

Psalm 119:20—*My soul breaketh for the longing that it hath unto thy judgments at all times.*

Psalm 119:24—*Thy testimonies also are my delight and my counsellors.*

Psalm 119:25—*My soul cleaveth unto the dust: quicken thou me according to thy word.*

Psalm 119:28—*My soul melteth for heaviness: strengthen thou me according unto thy word.*

Psalm 119:35—*Make me to go in the path of thy commandments; for therein do I delight.*

Psalm 119:50—*This is my comfort in my affliction: for thy word hath quickened me.*

Psalm 119:54—*Thy statutes have been my songs in the house of my pilgrimage.*

Psalm 119:62—*At midnight I will rise to give thanks unto thee because of thy righteous judgments.*

Psalm 119:72—*The law of thy mouth is better unto me than thousands of gold and silver.*

Psalm 119:92—*Unless thy law had been my delights, I should then have perished in mine affliction.*

Psalm 119:97—*O how love I thy law! it is my meditation all the day.*

Psalm 119:103—*How sweet are thy words unto my taste! yea, sweeter than honey to my mouth!*

Psalm 119:111—*Thy testimonies have I taken as an heritage for ever: for they are the rejoicing of my heart.*

Psalm 119:127—*Therefore I love thy commandments above gold; yea, above fine gold.*

Psalm 119:164—*Seven times a day do I praise thee because of thy righteous judgments.*

Psalm 119:165—*Great peace have they which love thy law: and nothing shall offend them.*

David saw the Word of God as the source of his strength, his hope, his encouragement, and his comfort. One gets the idea that David loved nothing more than to immerse himself in the very words of God.

Understanding Devotionals

There is a plentiful and varied supply of devotional books on the market today. One type will explain an author's personal insights about a certain passage of Scripture. This type of devotional will take one verse of the Bible and elaborate on it for a page or two. The author will actually apply the Scripture verse for the reader and will accompany the verse with a story to hold interest. Combined with human nature, this type of devotional tends to eliminate the need for a reader to open his Bible at all or—worse yet—to think for himself. These devotionals alone will never be sufficient to help a believer grow into maturity. They might be educational for children and helpful in discipling new believers; but they should be used sparingly and only as a stepping stone.

The second type of devotional book endeavors to extract and explain what the passage of Scripture is actually saying. These devotionals specialize in giving you the interpretation of the passage, but not necessarily specific applications. This sort of devotional is hard to find in a typical Christian bookstore.

The best type of Bible helps will assist the reader in determining the interpretation or meaning of the passage, but will allow the Holy Spirit to apply the Word of God to the heart. It may be beneficial for the reader to ask himself application-oriented questions to spark some thinking about the proper responses to biblical principles. Regardless, it is imperative to let the Holy Spirit do the work of application.

The best help for understanding the passage would come from a Bible commentary, not necessarily a devotional. If you start with the Word as your base and then move to the commentary to shed light on the meaning, you are taking the right approach. A good rule of thumb for Bible interpretation says that there is only one interpretation of Scripture, but several applications. Ask the Holy Spirit to guide you in finding individual applications to your life.

The Need for Immersion in the Word of God

First Peter 2:2 tells us, "As newborn babes, desire the sincere milk of the word, that ye may grow thereby." Most believers would not like to categorize themselves as baby believers; however, the Bible says a believer's growth is directly tied to his immersion in the Word of God. In America Bible *ownership* is measurably high, but Bible *reading* is quite low. Only eleven percent of Americans read the Bible every day. More than half read it less than once a month or never at all.[12] I noted in chapter 1 that among professing born-again Christians, only eighteen percent read the Bible every day and twenty-three percent admit to never reading it at all.[13] Without a doubt, a renewed immersion in the Bible is needed. We are on the brink of Bible illiteracy in America.

Pastor Mark Minnick said in one of his sermons, "There are Christian people who hardly ever read the Bible voluntarily. And there are other Christian people who may read it, but not with any regularity. And there is a third class of people who do read it, and may have some regularity, but hardly ever do so with profitability. And if there is profit, it is primarily intellectual."[14] Compare his evaluation with the command of Scripture to the saints in Colossians 3:16, which is, "Let the word of Christ dwell in you richly in all wisdom." The word *richly* means "in great amount." The goal of the believer should be to have great amounts of the Scripture taking up residence in his mind.

Believers need more than the Word of God on the shelf; they need the Word of God in their hearts. Just before World War II, Darlene Diebler and her husband Russell had gone to New Guinea as missionaries. One day, the leaders of the Japanese army came into the Dieblers' little village and took Russell to an internment camp while Darlene was forced to stay in the village. Eventually Darlene herself was taken to an internment camp, hundreds of miles away from her husband. Four years of physical and emotional anguish passed by, but Darlene's foundation of genuine faith sustained her. She was strong in Christ even when she was taken to solitary confinement because of false accusations that she was spying for America. When she was first shoved into her cell, the thought went through her mind, "They can lock me in, but they can't lock my wonderful Lord out." The shock troop took her Bible during the intense interrogations. The only thing that sustained her was meditation on Scripture passages. As a teenager, she had spent hours learning great chunks of Scripture; sitting in a cold, damp cell, she saw its value. She endured starvation, beatings, and the news of her husband's death. When she was finally released, she returned to minister to the people of New Guinea for another thirty years. When asked about her time in prison, she said, "I have no regrets. It was a way to know God in a deeper way. He was always there."[15] Immersion in the Word of God makes a difference in the midst of trials.

The Bible itself addresses the problem of deficient exposure to and knowledge of the Bible. The spiritual depth of some New Testament saints was not what it should have been, and they are rebuked in Hebrews 5:11–13. The author describes them as "dull of hearing." He continues, "For when for the time ye ought to be teachers, ye have need that one teach you again which be the first principles of the oracles of God; and are become such as have need of milk, and not strong meat. For every one that useth milk is unskilful in the word of righteousness: for he is a babe." The author is berating them for being believers of the gospel who apparently have no clue how to apply the gospel to their lives. These folks had reached a plateau in their growth. It was time to grow up! Many

Christians have grown older, but they have not grown up. If you are going to grow, you must immerse yourself in the Word of God.

The *Alone with God* plan will guide you to read two passages from Scripture every day. The first reading will be for the purpose of knowing God as He has revealed Himself through His Word. The second reading will be more interactive, encouraging toward an actual prayer conversation with the Lord.

The Need for Focused Prayer

Prayer is perhaps the single most neglected spiritual discipline in the life of the believer. In the 1980s, seventeen thousand evangelicals were surveyed about their prayer lives. Keep in mind that these believers were attending seminars on prayer, so they probably were more inclined to care about prayer than believers who had not attended. However the survey showed that, on average, those surveyed prayed less than five minutes a day. Of the seventeen thousand surveyed, two thousand were pastors and their wives. Their daily average of time spent in prayer was less than seven minutes.[16] Prayer is usually the first thing to go when our lives get busy. How can we stop and spend time praying when the "To Do" list is a mile long? The command of Scripture is clear—"Pray without ceasing" (1 Thessalonians 5:17). However some Christians make an art form out of running errands without ceasing, watching TV without ceasing, playing without ceasing—but not praying without ceasing.

Prayer must be fervent and focused. George Mueller said, "The great fault of the children of God is, they do not continue in prayer; they do not go on praying; they do not persevere. If they desire anything for God's glory, they should pray until they get it. Oh, how good, and kind, and gracious, and condescending is the One with Whom we have to do! He has given me, unworthy as I am, immeasurably above all that I had asked or thought!"[17] If anybody could admonish us in our prayer lives, it was George Mueller. He never asked anyone for money, but God provided time and again. Reading his journals is an encouragement to any believer. He was fervent and focused. I share one excerpt:

March 17.

This morning our poverty, which now has lasted for several months, became exceeding great. I left my house a few minutes after seven to go to the Orphan Houses to see whether there was enough money to buy milk. I prayed that the Lord would have mercy on us, even as a father has mercy on his children. I reminded Him of the consequences that would result, both in the lives of believers and unbelievers, if we had to give up the work because of lack of money, and that He therefore would not permit it to fail.

While I was walking and praying, I met a brother who was on his way to work. I greeted him and walked on, but he ran after me and gave me one pound for the orphans. Thus the Lord speedily answered my prayer.

Truly, it was worth being poor and greatly tried in faith for the sake of having such precious, daily proof of the loving interest which our kind Father takes in everything that concerns us. How could our Father do otherwise? He gave us the greatest possible proof of His love when He gave us His own Son. Surely He will also freely give us all things.

If the hearts of the children of God are comforted and their faith strengthened, it is worth being poor and greatly tried in faith. Those who do not know God may read or hear of His dealings with us and see that faith in God is more than a mere notion. There is indeed reality in Christianity.[18]

If you are like me, your greatest struggle is keeping your mind focused during prayer. The *Alone with God* method has several prayer times woven into the format. I have endeavored to break up the prayer times and to focus them to aid you in keeping your mind disciplined during prayer. Prayer is too vital to the life of the believer to leave undone. John MacArthur writes that prayer "is the Christian's vital breath. The reason some Christians feel so fatigued and defeated is that they are holding their breath spiritually when they should be opening their hearts to God to accept the atmosphere all about them—His divine presence."[19]

The Need for Spiritual Discipline

Samuel Taylor Coleridge was an English poet and philosopher who was one of the founders of the Romantic Movement in England. He had great talent, and much of his work is still read today. However, he was undisciplined. William Barclay, a Scottish theologian, gives this critique of Coleridge.

> Nothing was ever achieved without discipline; and many an athlete and many a man has been ruined because he abandoned discipline and let himself grow slack. Coleridge is the supreme tragedy of indiscipline. Never did so great a mind produce so little. He left Cambridge University to join the army; but he left the army because, in spite of all his erudition, he could not rub down a horse; he returned to Oxford and left without a degree. He began a paper called The Watchman that lived for ten numbers and then died. It has been said of him: "He lost himself in visions of work to be done, that always remained to be done. Coleridge had every poetic gift but one—the gift of sustained and concentrated effort." In his head and in his mind he had all kinds of books, as he said himself, "completed save for transcription." "I am on the eve," he says, "of sending to the press two octavo volumes." But the books were never composed outside Coleridge's mind, because he would not face the discipline of sitting down to write them out. No one ever reached any eminence, and no one having reached it ever maintained it, without discipline.[20]

As a result of the Fall, we were born with a natural inclination to please ourselves. The Bible states pretty clearly that we love ourselves, we love pleasure and comfort, and we chafe at discipline. Part of Christian growth is learning to bring an undisciplined body and soul under God's control. In our world you will find many motivations for discipline. For instance, if you do not show up to work on time ten days in a row, you are probably going to be fired. That cold, hard reality should motivate you to get to work on time. If you constantly overeat, your health will begin to fail, and you will be motivated to change. However, most people do not feel the same type of motivation or accountability when it comes to disciplining their inner man. Because it is unseen, it tends to get neglected.

1 Timothy 4:7–8 tells us that exercise of the body profits very little, but that the focus of the believer should be to "exercise . . . unto godliness." Hebrews 5:14 says that we should exercise our senses to discern good and evil. This word in the Greek language is *gumnazō* which is where we get our word *gymnasium*. The meaning is "to exercise vigorously." We will never draw near to God if we do not become more vigorous in disciplining our spiritual lives. J. Oswald Sanders said, "We are at this moment as close to God as we really choose to be. True, there are times

when we would like to know a deeper intimacy, but when it comes to the point, we are not prepared to pay the price involved. The qualifying conditions are more stringent and exacting than we are prepared to meet; so we settle for a less demanding level of Christian living."[21]

This method is just a method, and keep in mind that a method cannot make you more disciplined. You need to find out what is crowding out your time with God and decide to make time for Him.

The Need for Quality Time

Often during college, I would feel lonely on special days such as Valentine's Day. I found myself desiring to be married, but there were no prospects in view (or none to my liking). So instead of being frustrated, I bought a journal and began writing letters to my future wife. One of my entries was from the diary of Jonathan Edwards. When he met Sarah Pierrepoint, she was only thirteen years old, and he was twenty. Edwards' first mention of Sarah was scratched on the leaf of one of his student books:

> They say there is a young lady in New Haven who is beloved of that Great Being who made and rules the world, and that there are certain seasons in which this Great Being, in some way or other invisible, comes to her and fills her mind with exceeding sweet delight, and that she hardly cares for anything, except to meditate on him. . . . She is of a wonderful sweetness, calmness and universal benevolence of mind; specially after this great God has manifested himself to her mind. She will sometimes go about from place to place, singing sweetly; and seems to be always full of joy and pleasure; and no one knows for what. She loves to be alone, walking in the fields and groves, and seems to have some one invisible always conversing with her.[22]

About a year after writing that out, I met my wife, Jennifer. Right away I knew she was special. We got to know each other through an incident where her brother Josh fell from a tree and broke his back. We met in an ICU unit and slipped out to the waiting room to pray for him. When she started to pray, I could tell she spent quality time with her God. The depth of her passion and feelings for God were evident.

The week before our wedding, I read through the journal before giving it to her as a gift. The words of Edwards made me smile as I realized

I was about to marry a girl very much like Sarah. Her quality time with God over the years made her into a godly jewel. (Now, my wife was also a fan of Sarah Edwards. During our engagement, she photocopied sections of a book titled *Marriage to a Difficult Man: The Uncommon Union of Jonathan and Sarah Edwards*. But that's a different story.)

We must redeem the time and discipline ourselves to cultivate a relationship with Christ through His Word. A busy schedule can prove to be the most menacing enemy of a friendship with God. Time becomes our most precious commodity. However, Ephesians 5:16 commands us to be "redeeming the time, because the days are evil." *To redeem* means "to buy back." Many Christians seem to have sold all their time to lesser interests. You must take control of your schedule so that you can spend quality time with the Lord. Even the perfect, sinless Christ took time to converse with God the Father. Matthew 14:23 says, "He went up into a mountain apart to pray: and when the evening was come, he was there alone." Hank Hannegraf, a Christian apologist, says that "if you spend time in the secret place, you will exude peace in the midst of life's storms. If you do not, you will be a poster child for busy-anity rather than Christianity."[23]

The *Alone with God* method is divided up so that you can start out by spending twenty or thirty minutes in your quiet time. But ideally, after developing some consistency, you will be able to spend longer and longer periods of time with the Lord.

The Need to Plan

My physical exercise program encouraged me to plan my routine before I start. I wrote out every lift and what weights I would use. It took about five minutes, but it was well worth it. I walked into the routine excited about the opportunity to meet my goals and to have a worthwhile workout. As I saw the weeks go by and my strength increase, I was encouraged by the progress. I am convinced the same thing should occur in my walk with God. Many families in America have retirement plans, vacation plans, weekend plans, and vocational plans. We need to plan for our spiritual development too.

I am amazed at the amount of preparation reflected in the Old Testament concerning worship. In Genesis you see the patriarchs taking time to build altars. In Exodus you see the preparation to make the tabernacle. In Leviticus you see the different plans for the special offerings. You get the idea that worship was not some haphazard display thrown upon the end of a busy day. God's worship, done according to God's specifications, was central to the lives of God's people.

The first benefit of having a plan will be that it prevents you from getting stuck in a rut. I was a youth pastor for five years, and I found that most of the teens did not keep a faithful meeting time with God. Even if they did have a regular routine, many were continually stuck in a Proverbs-only plan. Someone, somewhere must have told them that the book of Proverbs was laid out by God in thirty-one chapters to be the perfect monthly devotional guide. The truth is God did not lay out Proverbs in thirty-one chapters; man did. Even though Proverbs is inspired sacred text, it can become hazardous to your spiritual health to get stuck in the rut of repeating the same book over and over again while neglecting the rest of the Bible. Don't let lack of planning keep you from exploring all of the Word of God.

The second benefit of having a plan is that it will help to curb a wandering mind. Taking five minutes to plan your time with God carefully could help to eliminate one of the greatest impediments to a meaningful relationship—a lack of focus. The inability to concentrate can be a terrible discouragement. However, a carefully planned spiritual "workout" will greatly help to keep the mind on track. This method is an eight-step plan that is designed so that you plan out your daily quiet time before you begin. After trying the plan, you will see benefits of scripting this most important part of your day.

4
the
Myths

For years, I was afraid of the monsters under my bed. I was convinced that my windowless room in our Wisconsin farmhouse was the perfect hibernation place for monsters of all types. To make matters worse, I shared a room with my brother, and we slept on a trundle bed. A trundle bed is a compact bunk bed except that the bottom bunk rolls out from underneath the top bunk, leaving a huge black hole. And you guessed it; I slept on the bottom bunk. I would often sleep on the side of my bed farthest away from the black hole (in order to avoid the paws of any prowling beast). When I had to get up in the middle of the night, I would jump at least three feet away from my bed to avoid a swipe at my ankles by the lurking predators. It wasn't until I was finishing grade school that I realized that I was being terrorized by a myth. There were no monsters in my room; there were no monsters underneath my trundle bed; there were no monsters in my entire house. When the myth was abolished, I felt a new freedom in my room. Fear was gone, and I enjoyed a restful sleep.

I believe good Christians have fallen prey to several myths related to cultivating a relationship with God. Satan has created the myths so that believers don't spend time with God. Some well-meaning Bible teachers have been guilty of floating some myths as well. And still other myths can be a product of personal experience—the result of thinking our own thoughts rather than God's thoughts. Regardless of the source, it is important for believers to abolish the myths with the truth of God's Word and to enter their time with God completely free and ready to worship Him. Let's examine some of the popular myths believed today.

Myth #1:
You are the only one who struggles with daily devotions.

Truth: The vast majority of Christians struggle with daily quiet time.

I work with an addiction recovery program. We see several new students each Friday night with addictions ranging from cocaine to sex to bad tempers. I enjoy watching the newcomers. They do the same thing every time—they walk in the door, slower than most, and look to see if anyone else is there. It's almost as if they think they might be the only one, and, if they are, they'll do one thing: turn around and head out the door. One reason they come to our program is that they see a sign in front of our church advertising the program. They assume that (1) there are other people with the same problems, and (2) those people are getting help. The power of community seems to take over at that point.

I have noticed several stages of discovery people go through when they struggle to gain victory over something. The first stage is covering the problem. I have learned in ministry that people are often more concerned about their reputation than their character. Most adults would be embarrassed if their pastor really knew the shallowness of their walk with God; the very thought paralyzes them. They are at the church every time the door opens—true servants. So they work hard to keep up an outward exterior of a vibrant fellowship, but inwardly they are empty and hurting. We have a tendency to pay more attention to what *people* think of us than what *God* thinks of us. It's almost as if we see ourselves giving a daily account to others for what they can see, but we neglect the fact that we will have to give an account to God who truly sees everything about our lives. Mark it down—you will not get closer to God by simply covering the problem. Proverbs 28:13 explains that those who cover sin will not prosper, but those who confess and forsake sin will experience the wonderful mercy of God. Sometimes society looks down on addicts, but if they truly understood that the addiction is just the fruit on the tree of a self-centered life, they wouldn't be so quick to judge. How many of us are addicted to a self-centered life?

The second stage of discovery is realizing that others have the same problem. Have you ever bounced a check? I have. It's embarrassing. I remember the first time I did it. It was more than just one check. I made a royal mess of my bank account. The charges for each check made me hang my head in shame. My lack of responsibility as a husband made me feel terrible. I told my office group about this soon after it happened. Almost everyone in the room began to smile and shower me with comfort. Stories began pouring forth about how they had done it and with much more flair and flamboyance than I had. I walked out of that room feeling much better. I wasn't the only loser in the world. They were losers too, and they seemed to be OK. In the area of personal devotions, you don't have to look far to find someone who feels like a loser. Take heart. God says everyone struggles with it. You are unique and special, but not in the area of struggling with devotions. 1 Corinthians 10:13 says there is no temptation or struggle we face that is not common to all humans. Isn't that comforting? We're all in the same boat. The guarantee from God is one you can count on: If you struggle with it, others do too. So be honest about it. Chances are those people you are closest to struggle with the same thing.

The third stage of discovery is seeking help for the problem. I'm not talking about a professional counselor here. I encourage you to open up and be honest with those who know you best. I guarantee you'll begin to see the smiles on people's faces as they relay to you their struggles with the same thing. We need to seek help from God and His Word. Proverbs 6:23 says, "For the commandment is a lamp; and the law is light; and reproofs of instruction are the way of life." God's Word can help us see the way clearly, but we need help from other godly people as well. Ecclesiastes 4:10 says, "Woe to him that is alone when he falleth; for he hath not another to help him up." Few people have someone in their life that they can be completely honest with about their spiritual condition. As a result, many Christians run into each other on a daily basis not knowing they are struggling with the same thing. They simply go on as if they were scoring a ten in their personal relationship with God. Remember the Bible tells us our faults are commonplace.

The final stage of discovery is conquering the problem. Christ has given us power to change. Ephesians 3:20 tells how God's divine power is working in us. You probably wouldn't read this book if you did not want to conquer the problem. Well, there's good news! You can do it with the power of God.

Myth #2:
Quiet time with God is boring.

*Truth: Your quiet time with God should be
the most relevant and fulfilling time of the day.*

In order to abolish this myth, the first thing you must do is change your mindset. Some people see the Bible as relevant for the time in which it was written, but not for today. However, the Bible says in 2 Peter 1:3 that God has given us all things that pertain to life and godliness. The Bible provides the only accurate portrayal of the real world. I can make sense of this world only as I understand who man, God, Christ, and the Devil are. I see the world the way God sees it. Real-world living means understanding the world from God's perspective. In John 6:63 Christ describes His words as spirit and life! No other words can claim that power.

Secondly, some people see the Bible as a book of facts, but they need to see it as a manual for deepening their relationship with the God of the universe. The Bible portrays an accurate description of the historical facts that it mentions; however, it was not written simply as a book of history. That was not His intent. God intended us to use the Bible to get to know Him more. Jeremiah 29:13 says we will seek Him and find Him if we search for Him with all of our heart. We are not simply seeking *facts* about God; we are seeking to know Him personally.

People need to see the Bible not only as God's Word, but also as words from God to them. The Bible is personal. I attended a funeral where the entire message from the pastor was written from the notes the deceased had written in the margins of his Bible. I could tell that this man over the course of his life did not see the Bible as God's revelation to mankind, but rather as God's revelation to him as a person. Psalms 119:24 says, "Thy testimonies also are my delight and my counsellors." The deceased saw the Word of God as a personal book.

Sometimes it seems difficult to get started having devotions—especially if you have not had refreshing experiences in times past. You need to learn to engage in the practice of meditating on the Scriptures, and you will find your heart will begin to warm. The Psalmist had the same problem. He began his quiet time down in the dumps, and by the end, he was on a mountaintop, extolling the praises of God. I believe that a God-focus through Bible meditation will warm a cold heart and alleviate boredom. One author said, "Meditation is a mighty engine to kindle cooling hearts, and make them flame in fervency."[1] Only that kind of heart could say of the words of God, "More to be desired are they than gold, yea, than much fine gold: sweeter also than honey and the honeycomb" (Psalm 19:10). Perhaps you need a change of mindset as described above, or you may need a change of method.

Myth #3:
The Bible is hard to understand.

Truth: You will be able to understand something from the Bible every time you read it.

The Bible is a deep book. Scholars who have pored over its pages for years have admitted that they were barely able to scratch the surface of its vast truth. Yet I believe a new believer can pick up the Bible, read it, and understand some great truths out of God's Word. First Peter 2:2 explains that the only way for a baby Christian to grow more like Christ is by feeding on the Word of God. He may not understand to the same degree as a great Bible scholar, but he will get as much as he can handle at that time. Believing that some parts of the Bible are "meat" and some are "milk" has caused confusion. John MacArthur says, "Paul's metaphorical reference to milk and solid food should not be misunderstood. He's not saying that some parts of the Scripture are milk, while other parts are solid food. Rather, all of the Bible can be either milk or solid food, depending on how deeply you study it."[2]

I like to think of it this way. I announce football games for our high school, and I love the job. I played football in high school, and this job allows me to step back and reminisce. I do something at the games called "Football 101" where I instruct spectators on the basics of the game, aware that many know little. I explain what "downs" are, why yellow flags are thrown, and how to score points. I do this because I realized midway through my high-school career that my mom had no idea how the game worked. She was my most loyal clueless cheerleader. I learned that she was much more concerned about me not getting hurt than if I was leading the team in tackles. I desired to educate her because the more she knew about the game, the more she would enjoy it. I want each mom at our games to understand what her son does, how he contributes, and when he makes a good play. However, as far as understanding goes, the players on the field have a much greater appreciation for the game than their moms because they have practiced all week for the opponent, they know the players on the other team, and they have a game plan. When a good play is made, the athletes are thrilled because they understand the game at a deeper level than the average spectator does. And while the players and spectators enjoy the game, the coach appreciates good football more than anyone on the field does. He has studied the other team, he has trained his own team, and he knows each player's strengths and personalities. Chances are he has planned all year for these games. When the team scores, nobody on the field or in the stands has a greater sense of joy and understanding than the head coach does.

Our Bible reading works the same way. Every passage of Scripture has something for the "mom," the "player," and the "coach." It should be our desire to grow in our understanding of the Word so much that eventually we will graduate out of a "mom" level of understanding to a "player" level and ultimately to the "coach" level of understanding. The Bible compares these graduated levels of understanding to milk and meat. Newborn babies don't eat steak; they drink milk but will gradually learn to eat solid food. The Bible says, "Study to shew thyself approved unto God"

(2 Timothy 2:15). The more we think on the Word of God, the more we are going to understand.

The wonderful thing about the Word of God is that it has something for everyone at every level of spiritual growth. Do not be discouraged about what you do not understand. Be encouraged by what you do understand and challenge yourself to dig deeper throughout your life. The Bible has been compared to a lake—shallow enough for a child to wade in, but deep enough for an elephant to drown in.

Myth #4:
You should read your Bible through every year.

Truth: The quantity of your Bible reading is not as important as the quality of your Bible reading.

Have you ever seen a fountain in the middle of a park or a shopping mall? What about the one with a cherub standing on one leg with water pouring out of his mouth? The statue pictures the way some individuals read the Bible. People read several chapters of the Bible everyday to keep them on track with an annual plan, but the vast majority of the information can go right through them, much like water through a statue. Because of this, many people grow discouraged with Bible reading plans. Many Christian organizations publish charts that help keep people on track. Believers keep these in their Bibles for the first month of the year, and once they get to Leviticus their mind enters a traffic jam. They start having thoughts of desperation and of wasted time. They consume themselves with one question: how do I find the nearest exit ramp? I am not against Bible reading plans, but they are not the divinely inspired method for effective quiet times. Reading through the Bible in a year is good goal, but *reading* is not the goal; knowing and loving God is the goal. In fact, this may come as a surprise to you, but God does not command us to read the Bible. The command is to meditate. Reading is assumed. If we are reading and not meditating, we are missing what God has for us.

A better devotional plan is to take a smaller portion of Scripture and meditate on it. The Puritans used to say, "A student never does himself such wrong as when he reads much and muses little."[3] The Puritans were the masters of meditation. If they were alive today, they would urge us to read with comprehension and thought. Nehemiah 8:8 speaks about the public reading of the word of God. The verse indicates they "read in the book in the law of God distinctly, and gave the sense, and caused them to understand the reading." The goal is so clearly stated. We must understand what we are reading.

One Puritan writer wrote, "It is not the great and much reading that makes the scholar, but the studying and pondering what is read. It is not reading much that makes the knowing Christian, but meditating on what is read: reading without meditation is like swallowing meat without due chewing: that makes a lean man, so this makes a lean mind."[4] So, consider reading less and thinking more.

Myth #5:
You should spend thirty minutes with God every day.

*Truth: Your quiet time with God should be
the beginning of a daylong relationship with Him.*

I am a planner. I like to plan my year, my week, and my day. I have tried to learn from time management gurus how to squeeze more work out of less time. I have used the Day-Timer and now use a PDA. I enjoy looking at my day on my PDA and seeing all of my appointments laid out neatly. It's how I get "psyched up" for the day. I have to write two letters at 9:00 a.m., meet with my secretary at 9:30, teach class at 10:50, go to staff meeting at 12:00, make hospital visits at 3:00, and counsel at 4:00. Everyone and everything gets its time and place in my schedule. And I often put God in His time slot—7:00–7:30 a.m. That's all His. Just God and me. However, this approach is misguided. I should not treat my relationship with God like another appointment with a starting and ending point. I want to meet with Him all day, not just before my day begins. I want to walk with Him as Enoch did. I want to retreat three times a day to meet with Him like Daniel did in Daniel 6:10. So why close my relationship with God when the big hand hits the six? With God, my relationship continually exists—there is no ending. Psalm 119:97 says, "O how love I thy law! it is my meditation all the day."

I can establish a continual walk with God throughout the day by cementing a truth about Him into my mind. As I go through my day, I think about God, meditate on His character, and worship Him in prayer. My best friend travels around the country as an itinerant evangelist, holding local church revival meetings. We have been friends since college, and we are knit at the heart. He is always traveling, is in a different church every week, and works until about 10:00 p.m. every day. Access is extremely difficult, and sometimes it is limited to cell phone messages and quick e-mails. When we get two uninterrupted hours, it is great! We solve the world's problems and then some. I always hate getting off the phone with him. I'd like to stay on the phone because I retreat into another world. This person knows me, and I can be real. What a refreshing experience this is here on earth!

Yet the telephone, the e-mail messages, and schedules do not limit God. He is always accessible. You may have heard commercials advertising the communication systems in automobiles. These systems can do a number of tasks. For example, they can run a diagnostic test remotely, unlock doors, deploy air bags, and contact emergency personnel (just to list a few). Advisers are on call 24-7, at the push of a button, to give assistance to the car owner. Advisers will help you with any emergency need you may have. They advertise themselves as being always there and always ready. In reality, they are not "always there." You must be in the automobile or near a phone to take advantage of the program. God is not like that. He is always there and always ready at all times and all places. I can talk to Him any time of the day or night. He is there, and He listens. He knows me better than my best friend does. I can be real. This is intimacy, and it can be yours. Your relationship with God should not be just thirty minutes. For that matter, it should not be just a day, but instead for life.

Myth #6:
Worship is what you do at church.

Truth: Worship should be a daily experience.

R. A. Torrey, the globetrotting evangelist who was an itinerant preacher, talks about the transformation that took place in his life when he realized some things about worship. It was said of him that he "learned not only to give thanks and make petition, but also to worship—asking nothing from God, occupied and satisfied with Him alone. In that new experience, he realized a new intimacy with God."[5] R. A. Torrey had observed worship on a corporate level in churches around the world, but he was transformed by the idea that he could worship God on his own. According to one Bible dictionary, the term *worship* means "to bow down, prostrate oneself, a posture indicating reverence and homage given to a lord, whether human or divine."[6] We must learn to worship God daily.

We can get the mistaken notion that this kind of worship takes place only within the four walls of a church building. However, we are missing the greatest opportunity of humanity by relegating worship to weekend services. Some people view church as the place to fill their spiritual gas tank, to give them power to make it through another week. A truer picture is to view church as the place to get a tune-up of our spiritual engine. The fuel is our daily walk with God. Going to church is a celebration with other believers of the relationship we have with God. At church, we hear the Word of God proclaimed from the man of God; we take our full tank and minister to others out of the overflow of our lives. Going to worship God at church should be the continuation and culmination of a week of constant interaction with the God of the universe.

One of the primary methods of worship in Scripture is through music. David was the chief composer of music in the Bible. He composed songs, was a skilled lyre player (1 Samuel 16:16–18), an inventor of instruments (Amos 6:5), and a valued court musician (1 Samuel 19:9). He wrote many of the Psalms, which are outpourings of his heart to God. Music warms the heart and fosters an attitude of worship towards God, and I would recommend using music as a regular part of your daily worship experience.

John Piper says, "Worship is the highest moral act a human can perform."[7] The good news is we can do it all the time. Contrary to popular opinion, worship is not limited to a sanctuary alone. Believers who have a maturing relationship with God must become good worshipers of Him on a daily basis.

Myth #7:
You can never remember what you've learned.

*Truth: Journaling helps you retain
and remember what you have learned.*

David Livingstone was a medical missionary to Africa. He gave his
life to the cause of Christ. Throughout his travels, he worked at mapping
Africa, abolishing the slave trade, and spreading the gospel. We still draw
strength from this great man today because of one thing: he journaled.
He wrote out his thoughts, his travels, his worries and concerns, his
failures, and his successes. We are able to see Christianity "fleshed out"
because a man took the time to record what God was doing. He was
so diligent about this task of journaling that it is said of him, "When
Livingstone ran out of notebooks he sewed ancient newspapers together
and wrote across the type in ink made from tree juices."[8] I do not think
that the greatest benefit to journaling lies in the impact it will have on
future readers but rather on the one who is writing. Journaling has a way
of helping the writer discern, examine, discover, and reflect what God is
doing in his life. In other words, *we* benefit from what Livingstone did,
but not nearly as much as *he* did.

Journaling has a reputation for being a girl's hobby. However, more
men seem to be learning the value of writing down their thoughts. Christian journaling is recording God's working in your life—past, present,
and future. There are a couple of reasons believers should journal their
spiritual lives. First, it will help you chronicle the works of God in your
life. In the Old Testament, men erected altars to remind them constantly
of the works of God in their life. Your journal can be a recording of
spiritual "altars" in your life. It can be a reminder of victories. David drew
on past victories over the lion and the bear to give him strength to fight
Goliath. What has God taught you over the years? What landmarks do
you see as you look back on your life? Chances are you will remember
big things but may have difficulty recalling the smaller things. Journaling will allow you to write about—in a concise form and on a regular
basis—how God is dealing with you.

Not only will journaling help you chronicle the works of God in your life, but it will also help you to clarify your thoughts. Writing has a way of helping you to think clearly; it is another form of meditation. This is why we buy pre-written cards for Valentine's Day. Someone has written so clearly and concisely that we are convinced we couldn't say it any better. Sounds romantic, huh? The goal of journaling is to put into your own words what God is doing in your heart. While you do this, the truths will begin to take shape and develop roots in your heart.

Picture the legacy you can leave your children if you begin now with a journaling project. When they see what you were thinking, meditating on, and processing spiritually, they will receive great strength. They will see you had similar struggles and fears. This is a practical way to show your children that you have "set" your "hope in God" (Psalm 78:7). What a legacy to leave.

I would encourage you to start journaling and to make it a priority. You will eventually look forward to writing every day. You will experience the joy of seeing your Christian growth on paper!

Myth #8:
You are too stressed out to spend time with God.

Truth: Regular time with God will do more to eliminate stress and a hectic life than any other activity.

Thirty-four percent of Americans admit to being "stressed out."[9] Stress seems to be on the rise, and peace seems to be on its way out. I believe that if someone is suffering from stress, chances are they have not looked upward and inward for some time. Jim Berg said in *Changed into His Image*, "A person without peace—constantly agitated or restless— does not know God well."[10] Psalm 119:165 proves this when it says the person who loves the Word of God will have a life that is characterized by great peace. I believe the greatest cause of stress is a lack of time with God. One pastor said, "The quality of your Christian life, the strength that you have from day to day to serve the Lord, is directly dependent on the quality of Bible reading that you do. Everything in the believer's life is dependent upon his intake of Scripture."[11] A cure for stress is meditation on God through His Word.

When you think about it, everyone meditates. Just look at the car next to you at the stoplight. Chances are they are either listening to the radio or they are lost in thought. What are those who are lost in thought thinking about? I believe most Americans spend their daydreaming time dwelling on their problems. They are *meditating* on their problems. This is nothing more than old-fashioned worry. Berg says, "Worriers are skilled in the meditation process. They are meditating on the wrong kind of thoughts."[12] As a believer, you are not to worry but to cast your cares upon God because He cares for you. If you are going to succeed at meditation, you need to re-program your mental hard drive to allow worry to remind you to meditate on God through His Word. Let me ask you, are you meditating on the Word of God or the worries of life?

Myth #9:
It is difficult to walk with God in this wicked culture.

Truth: Walking with God is the only way live godly in the culture.

Many times, those who have caved in to the pressures of a wicked world believe this myth. Those who knew God well in Scripture knew how to be "in the world," but not "of the world." Enoch walked with God (Hebrews 11:5) over a period of three hundred years, and he lived in a godless environment. Noah lived in a world far worse than anything we are experiencing today and found grace in the eyes of the Lord (Genesis 6:8). The culture did not have an impact on them; they had an impact on their culture.

Don't get me wrong. A wicked culture will have an impact upon those who walk with God: they will be more sensitive to the wickedness. The more you look like Christ, the more you will stand out in the crowd. Hebrews 11 talks about biblical heroes who learned how to be strangers and pilgrims on this earth because they were seeking a better country—a heavenly country.

God never told us to retreat from a wicked world, but to permeate it with His light. Matthew 5:16 tells us to let our light shine amidst a perverse culture. The darker the night is, the brighter the light will be! Don't let culture have an impact on you; you have an impact on the culture.

Myth #10:
You don't have time.

Truth: You have added things to your life outside of God's will that keep you from doing God's will.

When we say that we do not have time for something, we are not saying that there is no time in our schedule for such an activity. Instead we are saying that the proposed task cannot be accomplished due to other demands that have already laid claim to that time slot.

Americans are too busy. They have said yes to so many things that something has to give. Usually we get done what has to get done, and the tasks that are "optional" get put last on the list and seldom get accomplished. It's sad for me as a pastor to observe in counseling that the average believer has fallen prey to the enemy by not spending time with God. He's last on the list and somehow, He never gets "done." Believers have been distracted by the pull of the world and have no time for God. This "lack of time" can be attributed to two great time-wasters: hedonism and materialism.

Hedonism is the belief that pleasure is the ultimate good and is worthy to be pursued. First of all, it is important to understand that pleasure in itself is not evil. Leland Ryken, in the *Dictionary of Biblical Imagery*, lists six God-given categories of human pleasure: nature, human artistry, family, romantic love, social life and community, and corporate worship.[13] However, pleasure can be twisted.

R. Kent Hughes in *Set Apart* gives four ways that pleasure becomes sinful. First, pleasure becomes twisted when we forget that all pleasure is a gift from God and imagine that it is something that we can have apart from Him. Second, pleasure becomes twisted when it becomes a pursuit. God tells us not to pursue pleasure, only to receive it. Third, pleasure becomes perverted when we consider it our right. Fourth, pleasures become twisted when they are overindulged. It's not just eating a memorable meal, it's when every meal has to become memorable. This twisting of pleasure has wreaked great harm on the people of Jesus Christ. It has caused a great inversion of priorities.[14] This priority swap has resulted in a lazy mentality towards the spiritual disciplines. Why pursue the disciplines, which seem a whole lot like work, especially when pleasure is available on every corner?

Jean Fleming says in her book *Feeding Your Soul*, "Pleasures can divide our loyalties and divert our attention away from God. The pleasures may be innocent in themselves, but they become dangerous when they are in competition with God."[15]

God has seemingly slipped out of focus, and the latest Carribean cruise has taken over. Now we are so busy watching our shows, going on trips, playing on the computer, and spending time with friends that we no longer have time for God. It's hard for discipleship to thrive in this environment. It's a true characteristic of lost people that they are "lovers of pleasures more than lovers of God" (2 Timothy 3:4). This should never be said of the redeemed.

Materialism is the second great time-waster. Whereas hedonism is the end result, materialism fuels the pursuit. We need money and things to bring us that pleasure, and so we pursue them with all of our might. And it's making us work longer hours, pursue promotions, and give less away. According to a recent report, the average American household credit card debt was $8,562. In 2001, Americans paid $50 billion dollars in finance charges.[16] Savings accounts are a thing of the past in a consumer-driven society. Why wait when you can purchase the pleasure right now? You would hope that Christians would have a different set of values, but studies show that Christians spend money—lots of it—pursuing pleasure. In fact Christians spend seven times more on entertainment than they do on spiritual activities.[17]

By default, Christians have little time left to be quiet and still before the Lord. The pursuit of money can cause many believers to work too much, accumulate too much, and spend too much time taking care of what they've accumulated. Thus time for God lands low on the priority list. C. S. Lewis said, "One of the dangers of having a lot of money is that you may be quite satisfied with the kinds of happiness money can give and so fail to realize your need for God. If everything seems to come simply by signing checks, you may forget that you are at every moment totally dependent upon God."[18] The Bible says in 1 Timothy 6:10, "For the love of money is the root of all evil: which while some coveted after, they have erred from the faith, and pierced themselves through with many sorrows." Riches are not evil; however, the pursuit of them is deadly, especially when it robs you of your time with God.

You must set aside time in your schedule for God. In fact you must say no to some things, or the schedule of your life will soon be out of control. Why is it that believers spend large amounts of time perfecting their golf game or their scrapbooks but seemingly put little energy into their relationship with God? William Penn said, "Time is what we want most, but what, alas, we use worst, and for which God will surely most reckon with us when time shall be no more."[19] At the great judgment day, I do not think this myth will be believed by our Creator. We may complain of a lack of time, but He told us to redeem it.

Myth #11:
You have issues with God that are irresolvable.

Truth: Christ is our example of forgiveness.

Oftentimes, our biggest struggles in life are with God. People struggle with Him on several fronts: (1) they have experienced an unexpected loss and they blame God, (2) they have had unfulfilled expectations and question the goodness of God, and (3) they feel guilty because of past sin in their life. Therefore, they feel that God is unapproachable.

Many people struggle with bitterness toward God and therefore really have no desire to get close to Him. Unless you take your hurt and release it and repent of your wrong heart, you will never get close to God. There is no hurt that you have ever experienced that Christ did not experience Himself. First Peter 2:21–24 says, "For even hereunto were ye called: because Christ also suffered for us, leaving us an example, that ye should follow his steps: Who did no sin, neither was guile found in his mouth: Who, when he was reviled, reviled not again; when he suffered, he threatened not; but committed *himself* to him that judgeth righteously:

Who his own self bare our sins in his own body on the tree, that we, being dead to sins, should live unto righteousness: by whose stripes ye were healed." The key to avoiding hurt is to look to Christ. He experienced every form of abuse, rejection, and undeserved hurt that we could ever experience. Yet He did not get bitter but realized that God was the ultimate judge.

In the area of guilt, you need to understand that humans were not built to carry guilt. Just as the warning light on your dashboard is telling you that something is wrong under the hood, guilt is God telling you that something is wrong inside your heart. He doesn't love your sin; He loves you. Go to Him and accept His forgiveness for your sin. This adjustment must be made, or a relationship with Him will never develop. Regardless of past sins, trials, or times of running from God, He awaits the sinner with arms open wide. God is a forgiving God (1 John 1:9). Do not let an inaccurate view of Him keep you from having a dynamic relationship with Him.

The Bible says that He loves us with an everlasting love (Jeremiah 31:3). God loves you, and He desires that you love Him. J. Oswald Sanders says, "Love is the self-imparting quality in the nature of God that moves Him to seek the highest good of His creatures, in whom He seeks to awake responsive love."[20] That is it! Responsive love is a relationship with God. It is God and His creature responding to each other in mutual love.

Keep in mind that God will not love you any more or any less as a result of having a more intimate relationship with Him. You are not going to undergo an intense period of spiritual growth and gain any more favor from Him than you already have. He loves you as much as He ever will.

Myth #12:
If you start again, you'll fall again.

Truth: Failure is not falling. Failure is not getting back up.

Talk to every Christian leader that you trust, and they will understand you on this point. Character is not forged overnight. But don't look at your past attempts with discouragement. Take heart from Proverbs 24:16, "A just man falleth seven times, and riseth up again." Failure is not falling; it's not getting back up. Henry Ford said, "Failure is the opportunity to begin again more intelligently."[21] Learn from your prior attempts at a meaningful devotional time and rise back up and do it!

5
the
Nuts and Bolts

In this chapter, I am going to describe the eight-step devotional method I have termed *Alone with God*. Keep in mind that there is nothing sacred about the order and this is not a magic formula. God is interested in fellowship, not formulas. I have laid out the steps in a simple-to-follow fashion, and I encourage you to try the eight steps for several weeks before you make any adjustments. After a few weeks, feel free to tailor it to your needs and your style.

You will be getting a heavy dose of prayer and Bible reading. The average American spends less than five minutes in his prayer times and less than eight minutes in Bible reading.[1] This program will help you to double the average amount. However, I believe you will feel the time moves so rapidly that you will be craving more time with God. Before I explain the eight steps, I would like to briefly explain some important aspects of a good quiet time.

Planning

Time and Place

I recommend that you begin by preparing a place to have your time with God. Pick a quiet place with good light. Do not lie down on your bed, or your prayer time could turn into nap time. You may struggle finding solitude. You are not alone. Susanna Wesley, mother of nineteen children, could not find a quiet place in her home. So, she would often pull her apron up over her head for her time of private prayer. John Wesley, founder of the Methodist church and her fifteenth son, said, "I learned more about Christianity from my mother than from all the theologians in England."[2]

Secondly, I recommend that you pick a time that will be best for you. Many have advocated the morning because people are usually more alert at that time. In addition, David mentions several times he sought the Lord early (Psalm 57:8, Psalm 63:1, Psalm 108:2). The nice thing about having your devotions early in your day is that the chances of getting distracted with other things is not as great then as it is later in your day. However, we live in a twenty-four-hour society where many people work in the evening and sleep during the day, and some people are just not "morning people" and are at their best after 10:00 p.m. The time of day is not as important as the quality of the time. It is vital that you nail down a specific time as your goal. Do not simply say, "I'll get to it sometime today." The chances are you will continue to table it until you are completely exhausted and are unable to give God your best. Take the time to give God the time when you can be most focussed and have the least amount of interruptions. Give Him your best.

The Use of Music

Music can be a great aid in personal worship. Jonathan Edwards said, "I have vehement longings of soul after God and Christ, and after more holiness, wherewith my heart seemed to be full, and ready to break . . . I spent most of my time in thinking of divine things, year after year; often walking alone in the woods, and solitary place, for meditation, soliloquy, and prayer and converse with God; and it was always my manner, at such times, to sing forth my contemplations."[3] Four of the eight steps in the *Alone with God* method include prayer. During prayer I encourage you to use music for worship and expression. Most people are not great musicians, but the vast majority of people appreciate music; therefore, I propose that you use music by singing, humming, or listening. For listening, I would encourage you to use some of your favorite recorded music. You will want to have your music player nearby and at the appropriate time in your worship, turn it to the song of your choice. With this format, you can think about the words using them as a prayer to God, or you can sing along with the music. It is important to plan your time with the Lord, because you will want to find songs that match your purposes during your devotional time.

Resources

When you begin your devotions, I encourage you to bring your Bible, a songbook, and an *Alone with God Daily Journal*. Other tools that would be helpful are a study Bible and a good Bible commentary.

Overview of Eight-Step *Alone with God* Devotional Method

One of the keys to this method is planning your devotions before you begin them. V. R. Erdman said, "We live in a restless, impatient day. We have little time for preparation and less for worship. We feel we must be active, energetic, enthusiastic and humanly effective, and we cannot understand why inactivity, weariness, weakness and seeming uselessness become our lot. It all appears to be so futile and foolish, without plan and purpose."[4] I would like to encourage you to plan your time with God just like you plan everything else in your life. I recommend taking five minutes to plan before you do anything. To follow the plan, I have created two pages to help you have a refreshing daily quiet time. The first page is the *Alone with God* Devotional Planner. The second page is the *Alone with God* Devotional Journal. The entire plan is comprised of these eight steps.

1. **Preparation:** Preparing your heart to worship God through prayer, song, or reading of a few pages from a Christian book

2. **Confession:** Acknowledging known sin to God

3. **Revelation:** Reading one passage of the Bible with the purpose of learning about God

4. **Adoration:** Prayers and songs of praise and thanksgiving to God

5. **Transformation:** Interactive reading and prayer of one passage from Psalms or Proverbs

6. **Communication:** Prayers for personal needs, needs of others, casting our cares upon the Lord, and claiming God's promises

7. **Meditation:** Journaling truths learned about God from the two Bible readings

8. **Application:** Journaling practical areas of life that need to be worked on

The first six steps are on the *Alone with God* Devotional Planner page and the last two steps are on the *Alone with God* Devotional Journal page. Before you begin your quiet time, plan your devotions by filling out the My Plan Today section of the *Alone with God* Devotional Planner page. This planning time should take no longer than five minutes, and the more you do it, the faster you will become. Once you are finished filling out the My Plan Today section of the Devotional Planner, you are ready to begin your quiet time. The Devotional Journal page will be filled in at the conclusion of your quiet time. Here is a sample of the Planner and Journal pages.

Devotional Planner   Date: _____

Preparation

Prayer ◆ Song ◆ Reading of a Christian book

My Plan Today:

(This area is to be filled in during the planning time.)

Confession

- Confession of known sin

My Plan Today:

Search Me, O God

Revelation

- Reading to know God through one Bible passage

My Plan Today:

(This area is to be filled in during the planning time.)

Adoration

- Prayer and songs of praise
- Prayer and songs of thanksgiving
- Praying the names of God

My Plan Today:

(This area is to be filled in during the planning time.)

Transformation

- Interactive reading and prayer of one chapter from Psalms or Proverbs

My Plan Today:

(This area is to be filled in during the planning time.)

Communication

- Prayer for personal needs
- Prayer of casting cares upon the Lord
- Prayer for needs of others
- Prayer of claiming a promise from God

My Plan Today:

(This area is to be filled in during the planning time.)

Devotional Journal

Meditation

What did God show me about Himself?

(This area is to be filled in after you complete the first six steps.)

What verse or truth from my two Bible readings will I meditate on day and night?

(This area is to be filled in after you complete the first six steps.)

Application

What did God, through His Word, tell me to do?

(This area is to be filled in after you complete the first six steps.)

Other Thoughts

(This area is to be filled in after you complete the first six steps.)

Time Schedules

The actual time you spend is approximately twenty or thirty minutes, divided into eight segments. I have mapped out below how I divide the time based on a twenty- or thirty-minute plan.

30-Minute Plan

1. Preparation-2 minutes
2. Confession-1 minute
3. Revelation-10 minutes
4. Adoration-4 minutes
5. Transformation-4 minutes
6. Communication-4 minutes
7. & 8. Meditation and Application- 5 minutes

20-Minute Plan

1. Preparation-1 minute
2. Confession-1 minute
3. Revelation-8 minutes
4. Adoration-2 minutes
5. Transformation-3 minutes
6. Communication-3 minutes
7. & 8. Meditation and Application- 2 minutes

This may seem overly detailed, however, I have found after teaching this method to hundreds of people that they appreciate the guidelines. I encourage those who begin using the method to keep track of how much time they spend on each step the first week that they do it. This will give you a feel for where you would like to make adjustments. Feel free to spend more time or less in a specific area and suit it to your own needs.

So now that you have your time and place and you understand the basic format, let's talk about what to do. I would like to spend the rest of the chapter explaining each step in detail.

In-Depth Explanation of the Eight-Step *Alone with God* Devotional Method

1. Preparation Step

Psalm 100:4 "Enter into his gates with thanksgiving, and into his courts with praise."

I began my journey on the World Wide Web with a 28k modem. I didn't even think it was slow. Now anything less than high-speed access frustrates me. When I finally make a connection after a long dial-up, the home page of my ISP is a welcome site. I usually take a few minutes to peruse the news, and then I plunge into the Internet pursuing my real objective for logging on in the first place. The first step in your devotional method is your *Preparation Step*. I liken it to dialing up, scanning the news, and preparing myself for time on the Internet. The proper entrance into your devotional time can turn average time with God into awesome time with God. You usually don't start bench pressing, or running your mile, until you warm up your muscles. The *Preparation Step* is the time you spend warming up your spiritual muscles. Do not start your devotions by whipping out your Bible and reading. Take time to prepare your heart. During this time declare your intention to obey God no matter what He may tell you. If every believer would do this, we would experience revival in America.

I encourage everyone to begin their devotional time with a prayer submitting oneself to God.

Samuel Chadwick said, "We are moved by the act of God. Omniscience holds no conference. Infinite authority leaves no room for compromise. Eternal love offers no explanations. The Lord expects to be trusted. He disturbs us at will. Human arrangements are disregarded, family ties ignored, business claims put aside. We are never asked if it is convenient."[5] Perhaps the greatest struggle in our spiritual life is being yielded to God's will. I enjoy hearing parents talk about their "strong-willed" child. If they could only see in the heart of every one of their children, they would see all of them have strong wills. Oftentimes, we feel that because a child is quiet, he is passive. Not true! Sometimes the most strong-willed are the most silent. The Bible is not silent on this subject. It says we have all gone our own way! Deeply ingrained in us is a desire to do our own thing, to be our own person. Yet the believer should be directly opposite of this. The Bible compares us to clay in the hand of the Potter (Isaiah 64:8). We are the clay, and God is the Potter. The question for us as believers is, "Are we moldable?"

An example of a prayer of submission would be: "God, I come to you this morning and my desire is to worship You. I want to do Your will. Please help me to see where I am asserting my own desires above Yours. I know that Your way is best. May I be content to follow Your leading and guiding in my life. Not my will, but Thine be done. Holy Spirit, open my eyes to what You have for me in Your Word. I will obey what You show me today. I want to stay focused on You. Please change me today. Thank you God."

Another aspect of your preparation could be reading from a good Christian book or incorporating some music. Listening to or singing a song can warm the heart in worship to the Lord.

Here is a sample of what planning out your *Preparation Step* may look like:

Preparation

Prayer ◆ Song ◆ Reading of a Christian book

My Plan Today:

Pray

Or

Preparation

Prayer ◆ Song ◆ Reading of a Christian book

My Plan Today:

Pray, sing "How Great Thou Art"

Or

Preparation

Prayer ◆ Song ◆ Reading of a Christian book

My Plan Today:

Pray, read January 12th in Charles Spurgeon's Morning and Evening devotional

Or

My Plan Today:

Pray, sing "How Great Thou Art"

Read January 12th in Charles Spurgeon's Morning and Evening *devotional*

I believe that in our approach we need to make sure we are bold and humble. The two may seem contradictory, but they're not. The Bible commands me to come boldly to God (Hebrews 4:16). I have all the rights and privileges to attain access to His heart. So, in other words, don't shy away from it. On the other hand, I must be humble in that I am not here to tell God what to do. I am here to get my human desires to line up with what He wants for me. He is God. I am not. The Bible encourages us to be "clothed with humility." God resists those who are proud in heart, but He gives grace to the humble (1 Peter 5:5). I believe God honors bold humility. "Humility is simply [man's] acknowledging the truth of his position as man and yielding to God His place."[6] It is only this attitude that God will bless.

2. Confession Step

"Hide thy face from my sins, and blot out all mine iniquities. Create in me a clean heart, O God; and renew a right spirit within me." Psalm 51:9–10

C. S. Lewis said that a recovery of the old sense of sin is essential to Christianity. When a believer regularly sees himself as he really is, it keeps him humble. The *Confession Step* is a time that demands complete humility and honesty before God. Jim Berg says, "We sometimes think we are pretty good people who 'mess up' once in a while. The biblical picture is just the opposite: we are all pretty bad people who do right only by the grace of God."[7] We naturally do not like to confess our sins to anyone and especially not to God. However, we must remember God guarantees our forgiveness. We have a sympathetic, understanding God in the person of Jesus Christ (Hebrews 4:14–15).

It is important to understand the basis of confession from the Bible. The Bible says in 1 John 1:9, "If we confess our sins, He is faithful and just to forgive us our sins and to cleanse us from all unrighteousness." The Greek word *confess* is *homologeo* which means, "to say the same thing." Confession simply means to agree with God about sins. I simply say to God, "God, I agree with you that what I thought yesterday was evil and against You. I agree that the anger that I let fester in my spirit was wrong. It was sin." I do not need to spend hours in weeping or self-torment. God wants me to simply recognize and grasp the fact that I missed the mark in my life.

It is important to recognize the dangers of living in habitual sin. God says that if I am harboring iniquity in my heart, He will not hear my prayers (Psalm 66:18). In other words, if you are unwilling to take this step, you might as well close your Bible and go about your day because your entire relationship is going no further than your own mind. Hank Hannegraf says, "While unconfessed sin will not break our union with God, it will break our communion with God."[8] Although we will never lose the position we have with Him as His children, we can lose closeness with Him because of our sinful departure.

Proper confession will involve resolving your sin problem with God and getting right with your fellow man. During this time, if the Holy Spirit brings something to your mind that you need to resolve, write it down in your journal and determine to do it as soon as possible.

Keeping short sin accounts with God will make this time brief. However, you may be dealing with a major sin problem in your life that you need to confess before the Lord. I suggest praying through some confessional passages in Scripture such as Psalm 32 and Psalm 51. Perhaps you are struggling with accepting the forgiveness of God. I would recommend that you read Romans 3:21–26 to remind yourself of the depth of the forgiveness of God at salvation. Sanders says, "There is no sin so bad that it is impossible for the sinner to be cleansed from the guilt and pollution that would forbid continuing intimacy with God."[9]

I believe if your heart is open to the Holy Spirit, He will show you all the unconfessed sin in your life. However, you may not understand what the Bible calls sin. As J. Oswald Sanders says, "We each have endless capacity for self-deception and are notoriously biased in our own favor."[10] The appendix includes a list of sins found in the Bible (see pp. 120–21). Occasionally I read the list praying, "Search me, O God," asking Him to show me an area where I have missed the mark in my life. Every time I have used the list, I have never gotten through it without the Lord bringing something to my attention. Self-examination is a crucial discipline.

David takes the brunt of a lot of criticism due to his horrible sin recorded in Scripture. However, he penned some of the most wonderful penitential Psalms that serve as a great example of true repentance (see p. 122). If he became famous for an atrocious sin, he has been even more revered for the transparency and genuineness of his repentance. David is a model for us of how to get right with God. Your confession should culminate with praising God for the forgiveness that He has already granted by His death on the cross. As Sanders says, "God never leaves a penitential sinner in the dust."[11]

On your Devotional Planner page, I have put the words "Search Me, O God" into the regular planning space. I did this because nobody wants to write out their sins in a journal. However, this should be a daily reminder for you to allow God to search your heart.

Confession

- Confession of known sin

My Plan Today:

Search Me, O God

3. Revelation Step

"Then shalt thou understand the fear of the Lord, and find the knowledge of God." Proverbs 2:5

The *Revelation Step* involves reading God's revelation to us, the Bible. We read it so that God will show Himself to us through the Word. God's specific revelation to mankind is all contained in the Bible. There is no need for further revelation. However, sometimes we approach the Bible with the attitude that we know all there is to know about God. Nothing could be further from the truth. My college president instructed us to build our knowledge of God by making a "Biography of God." After reading a Bible passage in our quiet time, we would write down the main facet of God's character that impressed us. Since all Scripture points to Him in some way, every passage echoes His heartbeat. Proverbs 2:5 instructs us to "find the knowledge of God." During your *Revelation Step*, you are endeavoring to find God in the passage. As you are reading, ask yourself the question, "What is God trying to show me about Himself?" Sometimes I have called this step my "Knowing God Reading."

The good news is that you have a Helper for this step. You may have trouble in your reading because you feel like your heart has not been warmed in a long time. The question is, "What makes a cold heart become warm?" You only need to look at the passage (Luke 24) where Christ appeared to two men on the road to Emmaus. After Christ showed them the Scriptures, they said that their hearts burned within them. So there is your answer. The difference between their earlier exposures to the Word and their recent experience is that a member of the Godhead opened the Bible and explained it to them. As a result, their hearts were opened as well. The great news is that we have a member of the Godhead living inside us—the Holy Spirit. In John 16, Christ tells the disciples that He will soon be leaving but that the Holy Spirit will come and guide them into all truth. This was not a promise limited to the apostles. This teaching ministry of the Holy Spirit is available to all believers today. Knowing that you have the Holy Spirit as your "Reading Guide" should change the way you read the Bible. It will move you away from a fact-oriented, intellectual approach to one that desires to see Christ in every passage. The job of the Holy Spirit is to glorify Christ (John 16:14). He will bring Christ out of every passage of Scripture. We should pray as the Psalmist did, "Open thou mine eyes, that I may behold wondrous things out of thy law." (Psalm 119:18)

The first step in this phase is to pick your Bible book study and to move systematically through the book, journaling your thoughts about God. I started out *Alone with God* by studying the book of Acts. Each day I picked a chapter and began to chronicle what I learned and added to my Biography of God. After you complete this step in your quiet time, a space is provided on the Devotional Journal page for you to write out what God showed you about Himself.

I divided the Bible into three sections in the appendix for you: Easy, Moderate, and Difficult (see p. 123). Those categories will help you choose a book appropriate to the level of difficulty you desire at this stage of your spiritual life. If you have not had a regular devotional time with God, I suggest you start with the easy books. If you have never read the Bible systematically, I have marked the books that would be best for you to begin with. However, if you are a lifelong Bible student, I suggest the difficult books. After you complete one book, choose another one and continue to learn and journal about your great God. If you would like some Bible helps to aid your understanding, I recommend the use of some Bible commentaries or a good study Bible.

On your Devotional Planner page, write your reading for the day in the space provided as shown below.

Revelation

• Reading to know God through one Bible passage

My Plan Today:

Matthew 14

Keep in mind this step is only ten minutes long in the thirty minute plan. So, if you are going to read the Bible and a commentary at the same time, you will have to take smaller sections of Scripture. Feel free to extend this part of devotions.

Remember that the most important thing to glean from a passage is an insight into the person and character of God. A. W. Tozer said in his classic work, *The Knowledge of the Holy*, that "what comes to mind when you think about God is the most important thing about you."[12] I couldn't agree more. When your view of God changes to line up with the picture that the Bible gives of Him, your life will be changed! I like what Paul yearns for in Philippians 3:10. He says, "That I may know Him." You are endeavoring to learn to think as God thinks and to act as Christ would act. Our greatest joy and greatest fulfillment will be getting to know God. Your relationship with God will deepen as your knowledge of Him grows.

4. Adoration Step

"By Him therefore let us offer the sacrifice of praise to God continually, that is, the fruit of our lips giving thanks to His name." Hebrews 13:15

The *Adoration Step* could be perhaps the most refreshing part of your devotional time. Ten minutes ago, you entered His throne room. You opened the Word of God to let Him speak to you. He has just shown you something about Himself that He wanted you to see today. Now, it is your opportunity to talk back to the Lord and adore Him. You do this through offering Him praise and thanksgiving.

Praise is recognizing God for Who He is. Praising the Lord is a command from God. It is the most often mentioned command in the Bible. God knows we are naturally self-centered. We are thrilled to hear people praise us. However, regular praise centered on the character of God will help us place God in His proper place and ourselves in ours. David was a man after God's own heart, and he wrote more praise to God than any other Bible author. A reading of the Psalms will convince you that a praising heart maintains a proper view of God in one's life.

How does someone praise God? I traveled in evangelism with an evangelist named Steve Pettit. He talks in a booklet he wrote about using the names of God to praise Him. He says, "Often when I am discouraged and my cup is empty, I praise God for Who He is, and I say, *'Jehovah-Shammah—the Lord our presence. Oh Lord, I need your presence. You are Jehovah-Shammah. You are my God. You are here. You will never leave me nor forsake me. The Lord is with thee always, even unto the end of the world. Amen.'* Before ten minutes have passed, I sense the wonderful presence of the Lord."[13] I have included a list of the names of God in the appendix (see pp. 124–128). During this step, pray through a couple of these each day.

Thanksgiving is thanking God for what He has done. Thanksgiving is also a regular theme throughout Scripture. Thanksgiving is offered for everything including:

- Deliverance from affliction (Jonah 2:9)
- God's provision (2 Corinthians 9:11)
- Food (1 Timothy 4:3)
- Deliverance from enemies (2 Samuel 22:50)
- God's goodness (1 Chronicles 16:34)
- God's mercy (1 Chronicles 16:41)
- God's holiness (Psalm 30:4)
- God's works (Psalm 105:1)
- Wisdom (Daniel 2:23)
- Answered prayer (John 11:41)
- Other believers (Romans 1:8; Philippians 1:3; 2 Thessalonians 1:3)

The Bible says, "In everything give thanks" (1 Thessalonians 5:18). Bible characters usually thanked God for how He worked in their lives, whether it was delivering Noah's family from destruction or delivering David from the hand of the enemy. During your adoration time, continually thank God for His actions on your behalf. A grateful heart is a happy heart.

On the practical side, I begin my *Adoration Step* by verbalizing my praise to Him for what He has shown me in the Word about Himself today during the *Revelation Step*. Then I praise God for Who He is. Perhaps some aspect of God's character like His omnipresence has comforted me recently. I can praise Him for that. Praise can also take the form of praying through the names of God. After praise, I begin to thank Him. You can thank Him for what He has done in the past for you, for the world, or for His people. You should thank Him for salvation. You thank Him for what He has done throughout history or just yesterday in your personal life.

This is a perfect place to interject music into your devotions. There are countless songs of praise to listen to, sing, or meditate on. I have included a section in the appendix for you to create a song index of Praise and Thanksgiving songs (see pp. 118–19). If you do not know many songs, contact the music leader at your church to help you. A good songbook usually has an appendix where the songs are sorted topically, and this can be a great help.

Here is a sample of how the Devotional Planner could look as you plan out this step.

Adoration

- Prayer and songs of praise
- Prayer and songs of thanksgiving
- Praying the names of God

My Plan Today:

Praise Him for what I learned in my Revelation Step

Pray names of God 1–2 (see appendix, page 124)

Prayer of thanksgiving for provision

Sing "Amazing Grace" and thank God for His great salvation

A sample narrative of your *Adoration Step* could look something like this:

"Dear God, I praise You because of what I saw about You in the Word today. I saw You ponder the death of John the Baptist. I saw You show compassion on the multitude at a time of physical exhaustion. You were the greatest servant. God, I have looked at Your great names this morning. You are my Father. I praise You for being a dad to me. I know that You love me and care for me more than my own father ever could. God, I also praise You for being a forgiving God. I do not know where I would be if I had not experienced Your great forgiveness. Nothing is more comforting to me than knowing that You have forgiven my sins. God, I praise You, but I also thank You. I thank You for the daily blessings in my life. I also want to thank You for providing for me yesterday. I did not have the money to fix the car, and You provided in just the right way and in just the right time. God, I thank You for saving me. I never want to lose sight of that wonderful gift. God, I thank You for bringing me closer to You recently. Thank you for being a near God."

"Amazing Grace"

Amazing grace! How sweet the sound, that saved a wretch like me!

I once was lost, but now am found, was blind but now I see.

Let me remind you it is important to plan this time so that your mind does not begin to wander, especially when you begin thanking God for what He has done in your life. It is very easy to unconsciously derail and begin thinking about people, plans, and places. Stay disciplined in your mind.

I would like to conclude by encouraging you to study great prayers and to pray them. Many times, our prayers can be shallow and repetitive. Look in the Bible for some of the various prayers of the saints of God. Personalize them and pray these to the Lord. You can purchase several books that will help you, but I would just encourage you to make it a personal Bible study. Also, I want to recommend another book entitled, *The Valley of Vision*. It is a collection of prayers of several Puritans. Just praying these prayers to the Lord will strengthen your prayer life and your vision of Him.

5. Transformation Step

"Be ye transformed by the renewing of your mind, that ye may prove what is that good, and acceptable, and perfect, will of God." Romans 12:2b

We are in need of transformation. The Bible says in Romans 12:2, "And be not conformed to this world: but be ye transformed by the renewing of your mind, that ye may prove what *is* that good, and acceptable, and perfect, will of God." Our thinking is what needs transforming. At the moment of the Fall, the mind of man suffered the effects of sin. We came into the world thinking wrong thoughts (Romans 1:21–22). Thankfully, after salvation, we have the opportunity to change our thinking. The only prescribed way to do so is to gaze upon the Word of God. Second Corinthians 3:18 says that when we gaze upon God, we are changed into His image. One way to change our thinking is to pray the very words of God to Him.

We are now ready to begin one of the sweetest times in this method—the *Transformation Step*. Sometimes, I have called this step my inspirational reading. The emphasis is placed on praying the Scriptures to the Lord. You will take a passage of Scripture, read it, and then pray it back to God. By praying God's Word, you are letting His very thoughts penetrate your heart and mind.

I recommend that you spend most of your time in this step in the Psalms and Proverbs. They are part of the poetical books of the Bible and make for great conversations with God. Once you have picked your chapter for the day, I would advise you to read the chapter slowly and to contemplate it or to try reading it responsively. All you need to do on your Devotional Planner sheet is to write in the chapter you will be praying through.

Transformation

- Interactive reading and prayer of one chapter from Psalms or Proverbs

My Plan Today:

Psalm 34

For an example of a responsive reading, let's take Psalm 34:1–4. The passage reads:

"I will bless the Lord at all times: his praise shall continually be in my mouth. My soul shall make her boast in the Lord: the humble shall hear thereof, and be glad. O magnify the Lord with me, and let us exalt his name together. I sought the Lord, and he heard me, and delivered me from all my fears."

My *Transformation Step* reading is a prayer that could look like this:

Reading: *"I will bless the Lord at all times:"*

Response: *"God, I want to bless You this morning. You are my praise. I want to praise You all day, at all times."*

Reading: *"his praise shall continually be in my mouth."*

Response: *"God, may I praise You continually, to my family, to the people I work with, to those I talk with today."*

Reading:	*"My soul shall make her boast in the Lord: the humble shall hear thereof, and be glad."*
Response:	*"God, I not only want to praise You, I want to boast in You. I am proud to be able to call You my Lord. I do not want to be ashamed to speak of You always."*
Reading:	*"O magnify the Lord with me, and let us exalt his name together."*
Response:	*"May I magnify You like the psalmist did."*
Reading:	*"I sought the Lord, and he heard me, and delivered me from all my fears."*
Response:	*"God, I am seeking You today. I know You are hearing me. You know my fears. Please deliver me from them."*

I encourage you to use this method to commune with God. It will warm your heart as you pray Scripture back to Him. Take the Transformation Reading Guide in the Appendix (see p. 123), pick a chapter in Psalms or Proverbs (see pp. 129–30), and begin to read responsively. You will probably come up with favorite chapters to read. Be careful not to read the same passages every day.

Psalms and Proverbs will take you through six months of devotional prayers if you read one every day. Occasionally you will stumble upon a passage in another part of the Bible that will serve well as a responsive reading. Jot down the chapter number in your Transformation Reading Guide (see p. 130) and use it as your passage for the day in the future. For instance, Hannah's prayer in 1 Samuel 2 might be a wonderful passage to add for future use.

This stage is where you want to focus on meditation. It will take your strongest mental effort. Do not rush it, and do not get distracted in the practice. When you become used to it, you will never want to leave this section out of your devotions.

6. Communication Step

"And the Lord went his way, as soon as he had left communing with Abraham: and Abraham returned unto his place." Genesis 18:33

Now we are ready to bring our requests to God. The Bible says, "Ask and it shall be given you." This is a direct command of God as it relates to prayer. Even in the Lord's Prayer it says, "Give us this day our daily bread." There is no doubt there is an emphasis on asking God to work on our behalf. Asking in prayer reveals our dependence upon God. John Piper says, "Prayer is the open admission that without Christ we can do nothing. . . . Prayer humbles us as needy, and exalts God as wealthy."[14]

Consider structuring your requests into the following categories:

- Communicate with God about your personal needs.

- Communicate with God about the needs of others.

- Communicate with God by casting your burdens and cares on Him.

- Communicate with God by claiming His promises.

Prayer for Personal Needs

In the first category, you are asking God to "give you this day your daily bread." This step is asking God for daily provisions, not necessarily just daily food. Make the requests brief. These should be at the tip of your tongue as they are probably the most common prayers of Americans today. Whatever you do though, ask. If we do not ask, we do not enact the mighty arm of God to deliver. John Piper says, "A prayer-less Christian is like a bus driver trying by himself to push his bus out of a rut because he doesn't know Clark Kent is on board."[15] The truth is, we have the God of the universe on board! So, ask!

I encourage you to keep a prayer journal. I recommend having two types of lists: An "Every-Day" list and "Once-A-Week" lists. I have included some examples in the appendix (see pp. 131–34). Your "Every-Day" list will have items on it you want to pray for every day such as your family, your ministry, etc. The "Once-A-Week" lists will be explained in the next section.

Make sure you keep your prayers simple. Do not coat your request in flowery words, because God tells us we are not heard due to our "much speaking" (Matthew 6:7). In fact, God already knows what we have need of before we ask Him (Matthew 6:8). So, get to the point.

Be careful not to measure the success of your prayer life by the number of requests that God answers with a "yes." One author says, "Prayer is not a magic formula to get things from God. Communing with God in prayer is itself the prize. The tragedy of contemporary Christianity is that we measure the success of our prayer life by the scope of our accomplishments, rather than the strength of our relationship with God. All too often we are fixated on our outwardness, while God is focused on our inwardness."[16]

Prayer for the Needs of Others

After you have completed your prayer for daily provisions, begin to pray for other people. This is commonly called intercession. Intercession is the practice of praying on someone else's behalf before the throne of God. Job constantly brought his children before the Lord (Job 1:5), Paul continually had others on his mind in prayer (Romans 1:9), and Christ prayed for others regularly (Luke 22:32). True love spends time bringing the names of others before the throne of God.

I would encourage you to continue your prayer journal and add people to your "Once-A-Week" lists. You will pray for these people one time each week on the same day every week. For example, I do not pray for my extended family every day, but I do pray for them on Mondays. Therefore, I will put them on my Monday list. Using this method will allow you to pray regularly for a number of different people and needs every week, while not neglecting those needs closest to your heart.

Some possible topics for your "Once-A-Week" lists are

- Extended family
- Friends
- Those who don't know Christ
- Co-workers
- Your church and its staff
- People you minister to in the church
- Missionaries to foreign fields

Prayer of Casting Cares Upon the Lord

The next step involves asking God to carry your burdens and cares. Almost every human being feels stress every day. Stress is the product of allowing the burdens and cares of life to be internalized and carried by you. Stress is like a cell phone call reminding you to take your cares to the Lord. Steve Pettit says, "Nothing motivates us to pray more than our problems."[17] Instead of internalizing our burdens, we are to cast them upon the "shoulders" of God. God commands us to cast our care upon Him because He cares for us (1 Peter 5:7). Hyman Appleman says, "Most people are carrying the wrong burdens. Jesus' burdens are light." The illustration below pictures the two kinds of believers. I want to encourage you to take your burdens and cares and cast them upon the Lord.

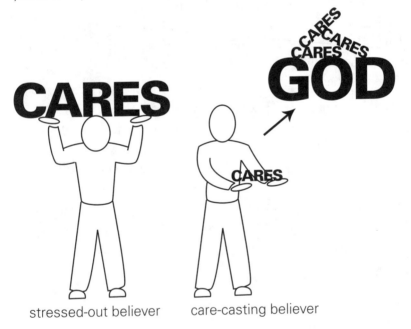

stressed-out believer   care-casting believer

Which one would you rather look like? Who is most likely to be joyful when they walk out the door in the morning? Become good at not taking your cares and worries yourself, but give them over to the Lord. He is the only One with the strength to carry them. By casting your cares upon the Lord, you are admitting that He has answers for your problems.

It is not a cavalier "I don't care" attitude; it is a dependent attitude of total trust in the Lord.

Prayer of Claiming a Promise from God

A vast resource awaits those who pray to God. He gives many promises in His Word that are available for us to claim. For example:

My Need	God's Promise
Wisdom to make a tough decision	James 1:5–6 "If any of you lack wisdom, let him ask of God, that giveth to all men liberally, and upbraideth not; and it shall be given him. But let him ask in faith, nothing wavering. For he that wavereth is like a wave of the sea driven with the wind and tossed."
A giving heart	Proverbs 28:27 "He that giveth unto the poor shall not lack: but he that hideth his eyes shall have many a curse."
Strength in weakness	Psalm 73:26 "My flesh and my heart faileth: but God is the strength of my heart, and my portion for ever."
Help in time of trouble	Psalm 34:19 "Many are the afflictions of the righteous: but the Lord delivereth him out of them all."
Deliverance from temptation	James 4:7–8a "Submit yourselves therefore to God. Resist the devil, and he will flee from you. Draw nigh to God, and he will draw nigh to you."

These are portions of Scripture that you can "take to the bank." They are promises made by the mouth of God. If you struggle in giving to the poor, trust the promise of God that you will not lack if you do so. If you feel like your strength is failing, trust God for His strength. He promises He will give it to you. Are you having difficulty making tough calls?

Ask God for wisdom. He promises He will deliver. God's great name is on the line, and He never goes back on His word. If He promises something, He will perform it. I have added some pages in the appendix listing the 100 Favorite Promises of the Bible (see pp. 135–42). Make them your own.

A sample space for your Daily Planner could look like this:

Communication

- Prayer for personal needs
- Prayer for needs of others
- Prayer of casting cares upon the Lord
- Prayer of claiming a promise from God

My Plan Today:

Personal—bills, mom's health, Every-Day list

Others—Monday list

Care casting—future job decision, conflict with family member

Promise—James 1:5

7. Meditation Step

"I have more understanding than all my teachers: for thy testimonies are my meditation." Psalm 119:99

You have now reached the part of your quiet time where you will write. Steps seven and eight are on your Devotional Journal sheet. The first section of your journal is your *Meditation Step*. Now the goal is to write down what you have learned in the Word through your two reading times (*Revelation Step* and *Transformation Step*).

The greatest focus of meditation in the world is God. From your two readings, write out on your Devotional Journal page how God's character was revealed to you. Your first part of the journal will be a section for you to record what God showed you about Himself. Start by asking yourself, "What did I see about God today in His Word? What was He showing me about Himself?" Write it down. Try to keep a God-centered focus in your journaling. Keep in mind that the part of His glory He showed you is probably directly related to what He wants to work on in your life.

Meditation

What did God show me about Himself?

God is compassionate. At a tough time, Christ still healed the sick. He was selfless.

God is the great provider. He was not limited by lack of supply.

Now, look over the two passages you have read and locate one truth, verse, or thought to think on throughout the day. Find the core truth and write it out fully in the journal here:

What verse or truth from my two Bible readings will I meditate on day and night?

Psalm 34:4 I sought the Lord, and he heard me, and delivered me from all my fears.

There may be some days when no verse really jumps off the page at you. Some have advocated continued reading until you find something to meditate on. However, we all have a down day every now and then. If you are just not "into it," you may be reading for a long time. Simply go to the appendix and pick a promise from the 100 Favorite Bible Promises list (see pp. 135–42). Use one of these as your meditation truth for the day. And there is nothing wrong with picking a verse from previous days to meditate on.

Next you will want to find some way to keep that verse before you all day long. This truth needs to find its way into your heart so that you can personalize it to keep yourself from sinning against God (Psalm 119:11).

You need to come up with a Meditation Reminder. This could mean writing it down on a 3 X 5 card or putting it into your day planner so that you regularly see this divine truth throughout the day. We will go into detail on the process of meditation in chapter seven.

8. Application Step

"But be ye doers of the word, and not hearers only, deceiving your own selves. For if any be a hearer of the word, and not a doer, he is like unto a man beholding his natural face in a glass: For he beholdeth himself, and goeth his way, and straightway forgetteth what manner of man he was. But whoso looketh into the perfect law of liberty, and continueth therein, he being not a forgetful hearer, but a doer of the work, this man shall be blessed in his deed." James 1:22–25

The final step of *Alone with God* is to write down what God has told you to do. This is a crucial step because now you get a chance to take action. The *Application Step* is the crucial link between learning who God is and changing to be more like Him. The Bible is very clear that we not only need to hear the Word, but do it (James 1:22). Chances are the Holy Spirit has brought some action steps to your mind. We can respond one of two ways to the Holy Spirit: obey the Spirit or quench the Spirit. Every time we refuse to obey His prompting, it is as though we are throwing cold water on the embers of a hot relationship with God. However, when you obey, you are enacting the blessings of God upon your life (John 14:21). The Holy Spirit may have prompted you to forgive someone, do a kind deed, become involved in a ministry, or work on your anger problem. Whatever He says, do it. I always get a kick out of the bumper sticker that reads, "Practice senseless acts of beauty and random acts of kindness." The good news about the Holy Spirit living inside me is that I do not have to do anything random or senseless. I can practice *sensible* acts of beauty and *specific* acts of kindness. Whatever the prompting may entail, it is important to write it down.

Application

What did God, through His Word, tell me to do?

I must realize that if God can walk on water and feed thousands with a small lunch that He can provide for my financial needs.

I need to selflessly serve my family by spending more time with my kids.

I must pray more! I must seek the Lord.

The last section of the journal page is entitled, "Other Thoughts". This is just space for you to write out any additional thoughts and contemplations.

Other Thoughts

You will be encouraged when you look back in your journal and see what God has really done in your heart in just one week. My advice would be to take one day a week to review your *Meditation* and *Application* entries. Keep these journals because they will be a treasure for future generations as they see the walk with God that those who lived before them had.

6
the
Covenant Friend

By now you might be thinking, "OK, so this lifetime relationship sounds like a great idea, but I know I won't be able to do it on my own." You're exactly right. Chances are if you have struggled with consistency in the past, you could use a friend to help you through the rough times. God never intended for us to take the spiritual journey without other Christian brothers and sisters walking alongside us. In fact, believers should have the closest friendships humanity can experience.

There are many illustrations in the Bible of spiritual friendships and even commandments to have fellowship with fellow believers. There's the story of the three Israelite friends—Shadrach, Meshach, and Abednego—who challenged each other to stand for truth no matter what the consequences might be (Daniel 3). Paul and Timothy had a friendship based on spiritual mentoring (1 Timothy 1:2). Of course Christ is the greatest example of a friend in that He gave His life for us (John 15:13). But the story in the Bible that tells in detail what friendship should look like is that of Jonathan and David. Let's look at their friendship under the spiritual microscope and see how they can be a help to us.

Friendship's Bond

Jonathan and David's friendship was born out of frustration. Jonathan was a commander in the army serving under his father, King Saul. In this battle with the Philistines, the odds were stacked against the armies of God. Armed with thirty thousand chariots and six thousand horsemen, the Philistines were ready to pounce on the tiny army of Israel. Jonathan grew frustrated with the lack of action and their impending doom, and so he took his armor bearer and snuck out of the camp. Jonathan explained to his armor bearer that they should go and attack the Philistine camp by themselves. Announcing his faith in God, he said, "The Lord is able to deliver us." They marched up the hillside, Jonathan charged, and he and his armor bearer wiped out twenty Philistines (1 Samuel 14:1–23). He had the heart of a warrior. Jonathan was the prince of the whole nation of Israel. He could have anything he wanted, and what he wanted was to display the power of Jehovah God and to silence His enemies.

A few chapters later, we read of a shepherd boy who was just as disgusted with a lack of action on the battlefield. While David was delivering food to his brothers, Goliath of the Philistines comes out and mocks God and challenges the army to battle. David, still in his teens, takes up the challenge and marches out single-handedly to meet the blasphemer. Just before he deals the death blow, he says, "This day will the Lord deliver thee into mine hand; and I will smite thee, and take thine head from thee; and I will give the carcases of the host of the Philistines this day unto the fowls of the air, and to the wild beasts of the earth; that all the earth may know that there is a God in Israel. And all this assembly shall know that the Lord saveth not with sword and spear: for the battle is the Lord's, and he will give you into our hands" (1 Samuel 17:46, 47). He slings the sling, hits the head, and the giant falls.

Afterwards, Saul calls David into his dwelling, and they have a talk. I can picture the young teen walking in, head of Goliath in one hand, sword in the other. The Bible doesn't fill us in on the details, but something happened there that changed David's life. Everything David said, everything he stood for that day awakened a desire in Jonathan. The Bible says that when David was done talking to Saul, the heart of

Jonathan was "knit" with the heart of David (1 Samuel 18:1). *Knit* carries the idea of being bound together in a league and made stronger.[1] Something happens when God-fearing people sense that someone else is passionate for God. Heart detects heart. One longs to share the journey of life with others who have a similar outlook. Jonathan saw in David a man of courage, character, and heart. There is no better type of friend to link up with. In spite of their differences in social status and family background, Jonathan and David shared the same spiritual fervor, courage, initiative, and loyalty. Aristotle described friendship this way, "What is a friend? A single soul dwelling in two bodies."[2]

Unfortunately many in our society today cannot fathom this type of unity because their friendships are based merely on physical attractiveness or social status instead of spiritual values and lasting character traits. As Gary Inrig says, "the essence of Jonathan and David's friendship is that it went beyond superficial attraction and natural attraction to spiritual attraction. Their souls were knit together. At the deepest level of their lives, they held in common a knowledge and love of God that had led them to stand side by side in love."[3]

Friendship's Quest

This kind of spiritual bond doesn't just happen. There is no magic fairy dust we can wave over another person and suddenly have the perfect friendship. We must diligently pursue the kind of sharpening relationship that David and Jonathan shared. There reaches a point in all relationships where a conscious decision has to be made—are we going to go deeper or are we going to stay on the same level? You probably have felt this when an acquaintance asks you a probing, personal question. You wonder, "Where's he going with this? This is different from the way we normally communicate." You have a choice: either answer the question and thus let your friend into the hidden parts of your life or dodge the question, refuse to answer, and keep the walls around your heart impenetrable. My point is, you are close to the people that you want to be close to and distant from those you want to be distant from. Friendship is a conscious choice, and it takes a concerted effort.

If we're honest, we'll all admit that we have blown it in some of our friendships. We have the best of intentions at the beginning. We promise that we will communicate with one another, get together for fellowship, and even pray for one another. Then when life gets busy again, our phone calls get fewer, and our prayers get consumed with other things. Somewhere along the way, we stopped pursuing after our friend. That day in Saul's chambers Jonathan made the choice to start a connection with the young man who had demonstrated such notable character, and he diligently pursued that friendship for the rest of his life.

There were some substantial obstacles that could have easily prevented David and Jonathan from ever maintaining their friendship. For starters, wouldn't it be hard to be best of friends with the person who you knew would take over your rightful place as the king? What about the jealousy that could have sprung up in Jonathan when people praised David for his military victories, yet no one stood in the streets and sang about the accomplishments of Jonathan the prince (1 Samuel 18:7)? Not to mention the fact that Jonathan's dad had tried to kill David on several occasions and even threw the javelin at Jonathan because he defended David (1 Samuel 20:33). Lesser men would have left David to fend for himself, but Jonathan had made a commitment, and he kept it in the midst of all the obstacles.

A study in contrasts in the pursuit of friendship is the difference between Jesus and His disciples. Jesus paid the disciples a huge compliment when He called them His friends (John 15:15). He revealed truth to His disciples that was hidden from others; He ate with them; He prayed with them; "He loved them unto the end" (John 13:1). He even called the one who betrayed Him "friend" (Matthew 26:50). The disciples, on the other hand, said that they loved Jesus, but they couldn't even stay with Him when He died. Their love and friendship came to a screeching halt when their own lives were at stake. Proverbs 17:17 says, "A friend loveth at all times, and a brother is born for adversity." Real friendship looks beyond the risks of getting to know the other person and concentrates only on the rewards of the friendship.

Even maintaining the spiritual disciplines we have considered in this book demands a serious commitment on the part of godly friends. It's risky to be transparent with spiritual friends in order to admit our own weakness. What if they think badly of us? What if they don't want to be associated with us anymore? What if they tell our faults to people in the church? The question comes back to the risk you are willing to take for the sake of pursuing the friendship and helping each other. No—godly friendship is not a genie bottle that you can rub and all your dreams come true. It's just plain hard work. The labor is all worth it, though, when you have gained not only a friend but also a fellow traveler in your walk with the Lord. "Without the risks of love, there can be no returns on love."[4]

Friendship's Pledge

So how do you start such a friendship? You do exactly what David and Jonathan did—you form a covenant. They saw each other's heart, and they pursued each other's friendship because they trusted each other (1 Samuel 18:3). They sealed their commitment to each other with a covenant. The word *covenant* in verse 3 is the same Hebrew word as the promises God made with Noah, Abraham, and David. "Covenant" could be translated as "league" or "alliance."[5] You have to understand, though, that in Bible days covenants were not entered into lightly. Both parties involved in a covenant understood it to be a binding agreement that could not be backed out of. Jonathan knew what he was agreeing to when he made this covenant with David. His word could have been his bond, but Jonathan went above and beyond that by committing to their friendship with a lifelong covenant.

Covenants pledge personal sacrifice. Verse 4 describes all the things that Jonathan gave to David as a confirmation of the sincerity with which he made the covenant. He gave him his robe. This gift showed David that there would be a shift in the royal authority from Jonathan to David. Jonathan also willingly gave David his armor. This was a picture of the military strength that was now transferred to this lowly shepherd boy. The next thing Jonathan turned over to David was the sword. This would have been a special sword because it was the weapon of a prince. From this moment on, everyone who saw David would know of the close personal connection to Jonathan. The belt was the last gift mentioned.

Jonathan gave of himself for the well-being of his friend. He was left with nothing that would instantly identify him for his position in the kingdom. This kind of sacrifice begs the question, "Why would he do all that for this friend when he might not ever see him again?" The answer is in verse 3, "because he loved him as his own soul." As nice as the gifts were, they were secondary to the heart behind them—the heart of unreserved love and an unyielding commitment to the promises made between them.

The story is told of Scottish soldiers who were captured by the Japanese during World War II. The prisoners of war were horribly treated. The soldiers would do random checks to verify that all the equipment used in daily labor was still in place. One day a shovel was missing. The commanding officer demanded that the shovel be returned or they would all be killed instantly. Finally one man stepped forward. The officer took a shovel and beat him to death. The officers then conducted another check of the tools. All the shovels were in the pile. The first count had been wrong, and a man had died as a result. An innocent man had given his life to protect the friends that he had come to love in that POW camp.[6] That's devotion. That's a deep commitment. That's covenant friendship.

Friendship's Allegiance

No one will ever keep a covenant with another if there is not a loyalty to that person. The loyalty of a person displays much of his or her character. Jonathan was a wonderful example of loyalty to his friend when it would have been easy to turn away from him. Imagine the scene. You and your friend have just had a special time when you have committed yourselves to the best interests and needs of the other person. Then a few months later your dad—a prominent man—says that he wants to kill this friend of yours. What would be your reaction? You've seen how angry your dad can get, but you don't know what he is capable of doing to you, much less to your friend. Some people would choose not to get involved because it could mean their death. Some people will talk about their interest and involvement in a person's life before the crisis, but they cower away in the middle of the crisis. Jonathan, on the other hand, was completely loyal to David regardless of his own peril. When Saul announced his plan to kill David, Jonathan was quick to warn his friend and to speak up on his behalf (1 Samuel 19:1–6). Saul calmed down, but just for a while.

At the time of the feast, David decided that his safety required him to be gone. Saul was furious. He started yelling horribly cruel things to Jonathan who had sided with David (1 Samuel 20:30). In his rage, Saul included the real source of his frustration—that one day David would take over the throne instead of Jonathan. Inrig points out that there are a variety of ways that Jonathan could have responded to his father. "He could have sold out, agreed with his father, and betrayed his friendship."[7] But even with this attempt to anger him, Jonathan remained loyal to David. He said to his father, "Wherefore shall he be slain? what hath he done?" (1 Samuel 20:32). Those two simple questions infuriated Saul to the point that he threw a javelin and tried to kill his own son. Jonathan's heart hurt for his friend. He couldn't even eat. Knowing that his own life was at risk, Jonathan still went into the field and told David that he must flee for his safety. They made another agreement that they would remain loyal to each other and to their families. At this point in the story, we as skeptical human beings are tempted to think, "Time will tell. A lot of people disregard their commitments when the hard times come." Time did tell, and for these two committed friends, their loyalty remained fervent for the rest of their lives.

We read about Jonathan and David meeting up again after David had lived in the wilderness for a while. "And Jonathan Saul's son arose, and went to David into the wood, and strengthened his hand in God. And he said unto him, Fear not: for the hand of Saul my father shall not find thee; and thou shalt be king over Israel, and I shall be next unto thee; and that also Saul my father knoweth. And they two made a covenant before the Lord: and David abode in the wood, and Jonathan went to his house" (1 Samuel 23:16–18). Even after enough time had passed for Jonathan to plan his takeover of the kingdom that by birth belonged to him, he instead planned how he could work alongside David—as second in command. That kind of loyalty is rare among people of any era.

Loyalty sees the need of the loved one and does whatever is necessary to meet that need. One of the easiest ways to test a person's loyalty is to observe him in the midst of personal crisis. In World War II, two soldier friends had been through everything together from basic training to being shipped overseas to fighting side by side in the trenches. One of the friends was terribly wounded in an enemy attack. He couldn't even climb back into his foxhole. Gunshots and bombs were going off all around the open field, but the wounded man's friend thought the reward was well worth the risk. As he started climbing out of the trench, his sergeant pulled him back in and said, "It's too late. You can't do him any good, and you'll only get yourself killed." Still the soldier climbed out of the trench, faced the explosions in order to get to his friend lying mortally wounded on the battlefield, and was himself gravely wounded. He stumbled back into the trench with his dead friend draped over his arms. The sergeant couldn't understand such an action. He said, "What a waste. He's dead and you're dying. It just wasn't worth it." The dying soldier said, "Oh, yes, it was, Sarge. When I got to him, the only thing he said was, 'I knew you'd come, Jim.' "[8] Jim demonstrated the loyalty that is necessary if any friendship will survive. Would you pass the loyalty test with your friends?

Friendship's Challenge

You might be wondering how this discussion on relationships with people fits with the theme of the book—our relationship with God. One of the best ways to strengthen your relationship with God is to find the right kind of a friend that will encourage you in your walk with the Lord. This is the function of a true friend. Look at Ecclesiastes 4:9: "Two are better than one; because they have a good reward for their labour. For if they fall, the one will lift up his fellow: but woe to him that is alone when he falleth; for he hath not another to help him up." When we stray in our spiritual journey or wane in our disciplines, our true, godly friends will be by our side helping us to get our eyes focused again on the character of God and the promises of His Word. That's what Jonathan did for David. Look back at the description of Jonathan's visit to David in the wilderness. Verse 16 of chapter twenty-three says that Jonathan "strengthened [David's] hand in God." One of the concepts of *strengthen* is to "restore to strength."[9] David was at a low point in his life—emotionally and spiritually—but Jonathan came alongside and lifted his spirits by shifting his focus and his faith back to God. We all have those wilderness moments when we want to throw in the spiritual towel and start following our own path instead of God's. It's exactly then that we must have a friend who is willing to encourage us in our walk and help us to get back on track with our commitment to the Lord.

Friendship can encourage us spiritually in several ways. We can be comforted in hearing a friend read the truth of God's Word to us. We can be encouraged by the listening ear of a friend. We can get the necessary rebuke from a friend when we sin against God. We can grow spiritually because of the accountability of a friend who is willing to ask us the hard questions. We can experience the unity of joining in prayer with a friend. We can go down a new path by heeding the biblical counsel our friends give us. We can be challenged in our steps of obedience by a friend who cheers us on to spiritual victory and shows us an example of that victory in his own life.

We've seen earlier in the book that we all tend to get derailed in our personal walk with God. Sometimes all we need is a little nudge from a friend. He could share what God is teaching him, and that could excite us again to study the Word for ourselves. We could spend time with our friends together in prayer. When Jim Elliot was in college, a few of his friends met together for the purpose of prayer. He wrote in his journal, "Several of my housemates and I have begun prayer together here in our den, and such times we do have! The first fruits of Glory itself . . . As soon as we hit a subject that has a need God can fill, we dive for our knees and tell Him about it. These are times I'll remember about college when all the philosophy has slipped out memory's back gate. God is still on His throne, we're still on His footstool, and there's only a knees' distance between."[10] That's godly friendship.

Maybe our friends could help us by asking the hard questions like, "What are you learning from your quiet time with the Lord?" or "What have you been praying about this week?" or "What are two things that you learned from the service on Sunday?" Maybe it's a little more personal like "What area of your life does God want to change?" There's an old phrase that says, "You don't get what you expect; you get what you inspect." If we are serious about taking steps in our relationship with

God, we must get serious about our friends "strengthening our hand in God."

Friendship's Legacy

Let's jump ahead a bit in the story of David and Jonathan. David was on the run from Saul for a long time. Every day was tense because David never knew where Saul or his men would be lurking. This went on for months. Then one horrible day David met a man whose clothes were torn, a man with ashes on his head. David knew that something was terribly wrong, for this was the dress of mourning. The man told David that Saul and his sons were killed. David wept in agony of soul for the loss of his friend. Then he wrote a song and asked the people of Judah to learn this song so it would be forever remembered. Notice the glowing description of Jonathan that shows David's thoughts about him even after all this time. It's called the Song of the Bow and it's found in 2 Samuel 1:19–27,

"The beauty of Israel is slain upon thy high places: how are the mighty fallen! Tell it not in Gath, publish it not in the streets of Askelon; lest the daughters of the Philistines rejoice, lest the daughters of the uncircumcised triumph. Ye mountains of Gilboa, let there be no dew, neither let there be rain, upon you, nor fields of offerings: for there the shield of the mighty is vilely cast away, the shield of Saul, as though he had not been anointed with oil. From the blood of the slain, from the fat of the mighty, the bow of Jonathan turned not back, and the sword of Saul returned not empty. Saul and Jonathan were lovely and pleasant in their lives, and in their death they were not divided: they were swifter than eagles, they were stronger than lions. Ye daughters of Israel, weep over Saul, who clothed you in scarlet, with other delights, who put on ornaments of gold upon your apparel. How are the mighty fallen in the midst of the battle! O Jonathan, thou wast slain in thine high places. I am distressed for thee, my brother Jonathan: very pleasant hast thou been unto me: thy love to me was wonderful, passing the love of women. How are the mighty fallen, and the weapons of war perished!"

The song of David's grief lives on to this day in God's Word as a symbol of the unending nature of friendship.

David's covenant with Jonathan didn't stop at his death. After David was anointed as king over Israel and Judah, he searched to find family members of Jonathan's that he might be able to help. A servant said that Jonathan had a crippled son. David could have easily just written a nice letter to Mephibosheth or even done nothing since he was now the king. Instead David instantly arranged for Mephibosheth to come to live in the palace. David took care of Mephibosheth as if he were his own son. "So Mephibosheth dwelt in Jerusalem; for he did eat continually at the king's table; and was lame on both his feet" (2 Samuel 9:13).

Even after all this kindness, David didn't stop there. The army of the enemy had stolen Saul's and Jonathan's bodies and had not returned them to the children of Israel. David himself went and gathered up the bodies and gave them a burial fit for the king and prince of Israel—the tomb of Saul's father. That was a gesture of true friendship because David didn't want Jonathan to be shamed even in his death. What a beautiful picture of the blessings of godly friendships.

We all could use a Jonathan in our lives—a person who shares our heart, pursues our relationship, enters into a covenant with us, sacrifices out of loyalty for us, encourages us in our walk with God, and never stops loving us. I want to encourage you to talk with others whom God lays on your heart. They probably came to mind as you were reading this chapter. Get together with them and tell them that you are looking for a relationship that will encourage you in the greatest relationship you can have—a relationship for life with God.

7

the

Secret

Nathaniel Ranew said, "Serious thinking is fundamental to all right doing."[1] He was right. And the most serious thinking that a believer can engage in is meditation. Not much is known about Nathaniel Ranew, but he wrote a book titled *Solitude Improved by Divine Meditation, or, A treatise proving the duty and demonstrating the necessity, excellency, usefulness, natures, kinds and requisites of divine meditation*. Only a Puritan could come up with a title like that! His work is considered by many to be the classic work on the topic. I will allude to many of his thoughts throughout this chapter. Meditation is misunderstood by many people. When the word is mentioned, people may think about sitting in a lotus position, eyes closed, palms up, focusing on who-knows-what. This and many other forms of meditation are all knock-offs of an idea that the God of the Bible initiated. In this chapter, it is my intention to acquaint you thoroughly with what the Bible says about meditation.

What is Meditation?

I want to start by giving you a brief glimpse of the mention of meditation in the Bible. Meditation is mentioned most in the Psalms. Here is a sampling.

Psalm 1:2—*But his delight is in the law of the Lord; and in his law doth he meditate day and night.*

Psalm 5:1—*Give ear to my words, O Lord, consider my meditation.*

Psalm 19:14—*Let the words of my mouth, and the meditation of my heart, be acceptable in thy sight, O Lord, my strength, and my redeemer.*

Psalm 49:3—*My mouth shall speak of wisdom; and the meditation of my heart shall be of understanding.*

Psalm 63:6—*When I remember thee upon my bed, and meditate on thee in the night watches.*

Psalm 77:12—*I will meditate also of all thy work, and talk of thy doings.*

Psalm 104:34—*My meditation of him shall be sweet: I will be glad in the Lord.*

Psalm 119:15—*I will meditate in thy precepts, and have respect unto thy ways.*

Psalm 119:23—*Princes also did sit and speak against me: but thy servant did meditate in thy statutes.*

Psalm 119:48—*My hands also will I lift up unto thy commandments, which I have loved; and I will meditate in thy statutes.*

Psalm 119:78—*Let the proud be ashamed; for they dealt perversely with me without a cause: but I will meditate in thy precepts.*

Psalm 119:97—*O how love I thy law! it is my meditation all the day.*

Psalm 119:99—*I have more understanding than all my teachers: for thy testimonies are my meditation.*

Psalm 119:148—*Mine eyes prevent the night watches, that I might meditate in thy word.*

Psalm 143:5—*I remember the days of old; I meditate on all thy works; I muse on the work of thy hands.*

The word *meditate* or *meditation* appears in the Old Testament from two Hebrew words—*hagah* and *siha*. The verb *hagah* is often translated as meditate, mourn, speak, imagine, or study. It is defined as to moan, growl, utter, muse, mutter, meditate, devise, plot, or speak.[2] *The Theological Wordbook of the Old Testament* says that it's basic meaning "is a low sound, characteristic of the moaning of a dove (Isaiah 38:14; 59:11) or the growling of a lion over its prey (Isaiah 31:4). It is sometimes used in mourning contexts, such as the moaning over the judgment upon Moab (Isaiah 16:7: Jeremiah 48:31). It is used in distress when the psalmist sighs and cries out to God for help (Psalm 5:1). The righteous can also *devise* or *ponder* a proper answer (Proverbs 15:28). In Psalm 19:14 'the meditation of my heart' is parallel to 'the words of my mouth,' as the psalmist compares his own speech with what God communicates in nature and in Scripture. Another positive use relates to meditating upon the Word of God; meditation which, like the plots of the wicked (Psalm 38:12), goes on day and night (Joshua 1:8; Psalm 1:2). Perhaps the Scripture was read half out loud in the process of meditation. The psalmist also speaks about meditating upon God (Psalm 63:6) and his works (Psalm 77:12; 143:5)."[3]

The second word is *siha* which appears as a noun and a verb. It is translated as talk, meditate, speak, complain, pray, commune, muse, and declare. It can be defined as to put forth, meditate, muse, commune, speak, complain, ponder, sing, study, talk, consider, put forth thoughts.[4] *The Theological Wordbook of the Old Testament* says "the basic meaning of this verb seems to be 'rehearse,' 'repent,' or 'go over a matter in one's mind.' "[5] This meditation or contemplation may be done either inwardly or outwardly.

It is used of silent reflection on God's works and God's word (Psalm 119:15, 23, 27, 48, 78, 148) as well as rehearsing aloud God's works (1 Chronicles 16:9; Psalm 105:2; 145:15). If the subject, however, is painful, it is translated "to complain" (Psalm 55:17; Job 7:11).

So *meditation* can be defined as to put forth, meditate, muse, commune, speak, complain, ponder, sing, study, talk, consider, put forth thoughts, moan, growl, utter, mutter, devise, plot, or speak.

One thing we gain from an understanding of the usage of these two Hebrew words is that meditation is not merely casual or simple thought. It is perhaps the deepest level of thought possible in the life of a human being. The word *meditation* then refers to thinking—muse, devise, ponder, study, consider, plot, put forth thoughts, imagine—and speaking—commune, complain, sing, talk, moan, growl, mutter, utter, declare, pray.

It seems to refer to deep, contemplative, conversive thought. J. I. Packer in *Knowing God*, describes it this way:

> *Meditation is a lost art today, and Christian people suffer grievously from their ignorance of the practice. Meditation is the activity of calling to mind, and thinking over, and dwelling on, and applying to oneself, the various things that one knows about the words and ways and purposes and promises of God. It is an activity of holy thought, consciously performed in the presence of God, under the eye of God, by the help of God, as a means of communion with God. Its purpose is to clear one's mental and spiritual vision of God, and to let His truth make its full and proper impact on one's mind and heart. It is a matter of talking to oneself about God and oneself; it is, indeed, often a matter of arguing with oneself, reasoning oneself out of moods of doubt and unbelief into a clear apprehension of God's power and grace. Its effect is ever to humble us, as we contemplate God's greatness and glory, and our own littleness and sinfulness, and to encourage and reassure us—"comfort" us, in the old, strong Bible sense of the word—as we contemplate the unsearchable riches of divine mercy displayed in the Lord Jesus Christ.[6]*

One Bible dictionary defines meditation this way: "A private devotional act consisting of deliberate reflection upon some spiritual truth or mystery, accompanied by mental prayer and acts of the affection and of the will, especially formations of resolutions as to future conduct."[7] Meditation is the most focused kind of thought that a human being can have.

Why Meditate?

Meditating on the Word throughout the day will change the way you live. I like to think of it this way. When an airplane takes off from Denver to fly to Los Angeles, it has a prescribed flight path. The goal of the pilot is to stay on that flight path until the plane lands. Rarely, however, is the plane ever exactly on the path. Many times wind and air pockets will force the plane off course. The pilot then uses his instruments to show him where he is. He makes adjustments accordingly to bring the plane back to the path. The instruments are his guides.

God's Word works the same way. Throughout the day, we can get off course from the plan that we set out in the morning to accomplish—to glorify God in all that we do and to focus on Him. Meditation upon the Word is the constant "aligner" of our lives.

There are also many practical benefits to meditation. One of these is that meditation produces spiritual stability. Psalm 1:2–3 says, "But his delight is in the law of the Lord and in His law doth He meditate day and night. And he shall be like a tree planted by the rivers of water that bringeth forth his fruit in his season. His leaf also shall not wither and whatsoever he doeth shall prosper." I like Mark Minnick's reminder that "we don't have a single spiritual malady that will not be met by faithful meditation in the Word of God."[8]

Meditation nurtures obedience which in turn produces spiritual success. Joshua 1:8 says, "This book of the law shall not depart out of thy mouth; but thou shalt meditate therein day and night, that thou mayest observe to do according to all that is written therein: for then thou shalt make thy way prosperous, and then thou shalt have good success."

Meditation makes you delight in the Lord. Psalm 104:34 says, "My meditation of him shall be sweet: I will be glad in the Lord."

Meditation makes you wise. Psalm 119:99 says, "I have more understanding than all my teachers: for thy testimonies are my meditation." On the flip side of that coin, deficient meditation yields deficient wisdom. Ranew says, "Little meditation also makes lean Christians, of little faith, little strength, little growth and of little usefulness to others."[9]

Meditation gives comfort in the midst of persecution. Psalm 119:23 says, "Princes also did sit and speak against me: but thy servant did meditate in thy statutes."

Meditation provides satisfaction in the Word of God. Psalm 119:97 says, "O how love I thy law! it is my meditation all the day." Verse 103 says, "How sweet are thy words unto my taste! Yea, sweeter than honey to my mouth!" Psalm 63:5–6 says, "My soul shall be satisfied as with marrow and fatness; and my mouth shall praise thee with joyful lips: when I remember thee upon my bed, and meditate on thee in the night watches."

The Meditation Process

Many may ask, "How do I meditate?" Meditation is summed up in 2 Corinthians 3:18. It says, "But we all, with open face beholding as in a glass the glory of the Lord, are changed into the same image from glory to glory, even as by the Spirit of the Lord." I would like to illustrate this verse with the following diagram.

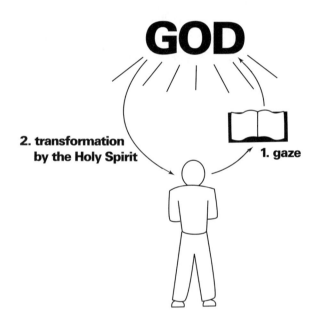

The Thought Process of Meditation

First of all, let's look at men's responsibility. My job in meditation is to behold the glory of the Lord. Daily I am to gaze intently upon the Lord, or in other words, meditate on Him. Meditation is fervent thought about God through His Word. Hebrews 5:14 alludes to the practice when it describes the way a mature believer thinks. It says that believers "by reason of use have their senses exercised to discern both good and evil." The word *senses* in this verse means "the capacities for spiritual apprehension."[10] In other words, believers habitually ought to train themselves to employ their spiritual faculties to help them judge between right and wrong. So, how does one train his spiritual faculties habitually?

Let us look first of all at how the human mind works. The thought process works in five stages.

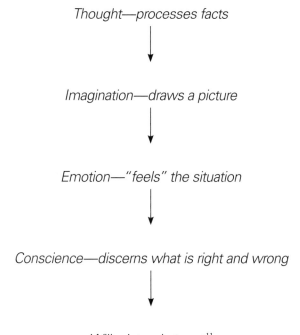

Thought—processes facts

Imagination—draws a picture

Emotion—"feels" the situation

Conscience—discerns what is right and wrong

Will—intends to act[11]

When we approach the Word of God, we need to proceed through all five steps in order to let the truths take hold in our hearts. We involve the mind, the emotions and the will. Let me illustrate this with the familiar Bible story of the Good Samaritan. To refresh your memory, in Luke 10:25–37, Christ encouraged a lawyer to obey the greatest commandments in the Bible which are to love your God with all your heart, soul, strength, and mind, and to love your neighbor as yourself. The lawyer then asks, "And who is my neighbor?" Christ responds with this story. A man is traveling from Jerusalem to Jericho and is beaten by thieves. Three men pass by, and only the last one helps—a Samaritan gentleman. He puts the injured man on his donkey, takes him to the next town, and pays for his care. He even says that he will come back and pay the balance that is left. Now when we read that passage, it should transform us when we meditate upon it. Let's see how my mind processes this story.

Thought (processes facts)—Man traveling down road, beaten by thieves, left half dead, priest and Levite pass by on other side of road, Samaritan saw him, had compassion on him, bandaged his wounds, took him to an inn, paid for his expenses.

Imagination (draws a picture)—I picture a bearded man in his midthirties traveling on a donkey down a dusty road. Five men come from behind a clump of trees. They knock him to the ground, take his money, and beat him. The men flee. The man is lying on the ground in extreme pain. I imagine a priest dressed in a white robe with a scroll under his arm seeing the bloody man and passing by on the other side of the road. I imagine the Levite, well dressed, hurrying to an appointment, registering disgust at the sight of the man. Then along comes a Samaritan. He stops his donkey, runs over to the man, bandages his wounds, pours in oil and wine, and lifts him onto his own donkey. Walking alongside the donkey, he transports the wounded man to an inn. When they reach the inn, the Samaritan takes out his money pouch, gives two day's wages to the innkeeper, and they carry the wounded man to a room. The man is laid down on a bed to recover. I imagine the Samaritan making arrangements to come back and take care of any additional cost when he returns.

Emotion ("feels" the situation)—I am angered that the sludge of society would prey upon a helpless man. I feel concern for the man as he lies there in pain. I gain hope as I see a man approaching. After all, he looks like a spiritual man. What? He's going to leave him there? How could he? Anger! But wait. Here comes another man. Maybe he can help. Hope rises again. He crosses the road and leaves the man! Frustration. A third man comes along. I can feel the despair in the suffering man's heart. Wait. The man stops. Finally, someone will help this man! Not only does he stop, but he bestows compassion on the man and nurses his wounds. I feel a sense of relief. He puts the man on his own donkey and walks beside the animal on the way to the hotel. They get to the inn, and now the man takes out his money and pays the bills. I feel the innkeeper's surprise at the generosity of a stranger. Now I know something is unusual about this man. I see gratitude on the face of the wounded man as he bids the Samaritan farewell. I feel the Samaritan's own genuine joy in giving as he mounts his donkey and heads back up the road.

Conscience (discerns what is right and wrong)—I realize that the thieves were totally wrong. They broke the law and inflicted human suffering. The priest and the Levite were wrong because they saw the need of the man and left him alone. If the man had died, they would have carried some of the blame. Perhaps the most grievous part is that they both appeared to be religious men who should have known better. The Samaritan was the example to follow in the story. He did everything he should have done and more. He sacrificed his time, energy, and money to help this hurting man. His schedule was not as important as the needs of this man.

Will (intends to act)—I will not steal. I will not harm another individual for my gain. When I see someone in need, I will not turn the other way. I will not allow my schedule to keep me from taking care of urgent needs. I will give of my time, energy, and money to help those who are in need. I will go above and beyond the call of duty. I will see everyone as my neighbor and, to the best of my ability, help them in their time of need.

Christ ends this great story by asking, "So which of these three do you think was neighbor to him who fell among thieves?" The lawyer guesses the obvious, and Christ says, "Go and do likewise." In other words, your neighbor is not the person next door but every other living person in this world besides yourself. So, go and be compassionate to them. Christ just opened the eyes of an exacting, factual lawyer and confronted him with his need to be compassionate.

The above scenario shows how a believer's mind might process a passage of Scripture if he really took the time to think through what he was reading. The question for you is, "Do you truly read the Bible that thoughtfully?" Or do you skim through the verses without any actual thought about why God might have included them in His Word? You will struggle to see Christ in the passages of Scripture without focused thought.

Meditation is fervent thought about God through His Word. Such a thorough approach to the thought process may seem like a lot of extra work, but it is never wasted. Not only is it worthwhile work, but the Puritans actually described this kind of thought as entertainment. They enjoyed the process of getting to know God this way.

The Source of Meditation

The diagram on page 98 shows the Bible. Second Corinthians 3:18 mentions the "glass" or "mirror" and the Bible is the mirror into which we look for an absolutely true account of Who God is and of who we are. The only trustworthy way for a believer to get a glimpse of the glory of God is through His revelation to mankind—the Bible. The majority of meditation methods popular today lack credibility because their sources are fallible. Sure, I can meditate upon pithy quotes by great scholars, but God commands me to meditate on the great truths of Scripture. We have been commanded to meditate upon only one revelation—the Word of God.

The Bible is multifaceted in its applicability to our lives. Not only is it the only divinely inspired literature on Earth, but it is also good for doctrine, reproof, correction, and instruction in righteousness. It helps me know the right path, where I strayed off the path, how to get back on the path, and how to stay on the right path. Meditation and the Bible go hand in hand. One without the other will not profit the believer. Jim Berg said, "Reflection without revelation equals despair. Revelation without reflection equals self-deception. Revelation with reflection equals dependency."[12]

The Object of Meditation

Move to the top of the diagram on page 98 for an illustration of 2 Corinthians 3:18 that talks about the "glory of the Lord." His glory is His "praise, honor, magnificence, excellence."[13] This means that I am to look for the unique excellence of God in the pages of Scripture. Ranew said, "Meditation is a peculiar visit made to the great God; a mind, a thought visit, as to a great friend, the soul, as it were, comes and saith to God, Lord, I come to see thee, I now come purposely to see thee, to spend some fit portion of time with thee, and I come for that high honour and observance I am infinitely obliged to tender to thee."[14]

Scripture is the source, but it is not the object of meditation. The goal of all Bible reading, prayer, and worship is God. Psalm 16:8 says, "I have set the Lord always before me." God must be my goal. Ranew said, "Meditation should be chiefly acted to see God, and to aim at glorifying of God above all."[15] All of Scripture paints a picture of God. Andrew Murray said, "You would be like Christ? Here is the path. Gaze on the glory of God in Him. In Him, that is to say, do not look only to the words and the thoughts and the graces in which his glory is seen, but look to Himself, the loving, living Christ. Behold Him! Look in His very eye! Look into His face, as a loving friend, as the living God."[16]

The Transformation of Meditation

We have just looked at what our part is in the meditation process; let us look at God's part. The Bible says that the result of meditation should be transformation. The Holy Spirit changes us into the image of Christ. The actual Greek word for *change* is the same root word from which we get our word *metamorphosis*. The present continuous tenses in this passage indicate that change is an ongoing process, not a one-time event. This kind of change is less like the flip of a light switch, and more like a caterpillar turning into a beautiful butterfly.

Change toward Christlikeness is the miracle of the Christian life. I cannot help it. If I meditate upon God, I will change to be like Him. Why do some believers seem so different from you? Why do some seem to have a closer walk with God? What is their secret? They have spent much time gazing upon God, and the Holy Spirit has spent a lot of time transforming them.

A. W. Tozer said, "Many have found the secret of which I speak and, without giving much thought to what was going on within them, constantly practice this habit of inwardly gazing on God. They know that something inside their hearts sees God. Even when they are compelled to withdraw their conscious attention in order to engage in earthly affairs, there is within them a secret communion going on. Let their attention be released but for a moment from necessary business, and it flies to God once again."[17] Those who meditate on God's word cannot help but be transformed.

The Progression of Meditation

The verse also says we are changed "from glory to glory." The passage could be read that as we meditate upon the excellencies of God, we are changed into the image of Christ by looking upon one aspect of His character and then another. Charles Spurgeon said, "Consider our Lord Jesus Christ in any way you please, and your meditation of him will be sweet. Jesus may be compared to some of those lenses you have seen, which you may take up, and hold one way, and you see one kind of light, and then hold in another way, and you see another kind of light; and whichever way you turn them, you will always see some precious sparkling light, and some new colours starting up to your view. Ah! Take Jesus for your theme, sit down, and consider him, think of his relation to your own soul, and you will never get through that one subject."[18] The glories of Christ are abundant. He will slowly reveal them to you as you study Him through the Word—from glory to glory.

While I was writing this chapter, I was admitted to the hospital because of a virus that attacked my heart. My heart muscle was damaged, and I was on my back for quite a while. During that time, an aspect of God's character that was displayed to me was His wonderful grace. I was confronted with the brevity of life and how my every breath was a gift of God's grace. When God is working in a specific area of your life, He is working to get you to see His perfection and excellency in that area. For instance, if you struggle with brotherly love, He will want to show you the glory of His perfect unconditional love. If you struggle with habitual sin, He will show you the glory of His holiness. If you have difficulty controlling your temper, He will show you His sweet demeanor and grace. As you meditate on the different facets of God's glory, He will change you to be like Him in those areas.

Ranew says, "Christians that least look at Christ, and least distinctly view him will make the slowest progress; and such as study him most, will have the easiest and most expeditious coming up to the main work."[19] What aspects of your character is God working on right now? What part of His glory is influencing you as you gaze on Him? In the book of Job, this righteous man suffers inestimable losses. Job loses his possessions, his children, and his health. He spends a great deal of time with his friends trying to discern what God is trying to do. God speaks in the last part of the book and gives Job a speech he will never forget. Job responds humbly to God as he sees God in a whole new light. He says in Job 42:5, "I have heard of thee by the hearing of the ear: but now mine eye seeth thee." Job sees facets of God that he had never seen before. This sight changes Job's perspective on his suffering in light of the glory of the Lord.

Meditation Helps

I want to give you as many helps as possible to make meditation a reality in your daily life. As I said earlier, meditation is the most focused thought a human being could have. How then can you focus deeply on spiritual things?

During your Bible reading, I encourage you to find one key truth that you can meditate on that day. You may read thirty to forty verses for your daily reading, but I encourage you to take a portion of a verse, one full verse, or several verses as your meditation truth for that day. It is the truth you want to internalize in your heart so that when the wild winds of the trials of life blow, you can have an anchor that will keep you moored to the right place. These truths are your spiritual food every day.

It may not be a verse. It may be a principle. For instance, it is difficult to find a verse in the passage on Abraham's call in Genesis 12 that would be a good verse to meditate on. However the great underlying truth there might be that God calls people, by His own divine grace, to do great things for Him. You can ruminate on such a truth all day to the point that the truth will never leave you. In the parable of the Good Samaritan you may want to sum up your thoughts by meditating on this principle, "Since everyone is my neighbor, I will obey God in loving them in any way I can." Or, if you prefer to meditate on a verse, pick "love your neighbor as yourself."

I believe that meditation must be regular—day and night—and it must be focused, intense thought. So I need to embed into my mind the truth that I am meditating on for the day. A few ways to focus your thoughts are listed below:

1. *Read the passage multiple times (ten or twenty).*

2. *Emphasize key words in the passage when you read it.*

   Love your neighbor as yourself.
   Love **your** neighbor as yourself.
   Love your **neighbor** as yourself.
   Love your neighbor as **yourself.**

3. *Interrogate the passage (using Who?, What?, When?, Where?, Why?, and How?).*

   Who am I to love?
   My neighbor
   What am I supposed to love?
   My neighbor
   When am I supposed to love?
   As I walk by the way, at all times
   Where am I supposed to love?
   Wherever a need arises
   Why am I supposed to love?
   God commanded it; He loved me
   How am I supposed to love?
   Unselfishly, immediately and beyond expectation

4. *Personalize the passage.*

   Jason, love your neighbor as yourself.
   Jason, love your wife as yourself.
   Jason, love your children as yourself.
   Jason, love your pastor as yourself.
   Jason, love your co-workers as yourself.
   Jason, love your enemies as yourself.

5. *Read it back to God responsively.*

"God, help me to love my neighbor as myself. I know that you loved me even when I was yet a sinner."

6. *Memorize it.*

7. *Write it out.*

8. *Say it aloud at every meal.*

9. *Visualize it as you slowly read it.*

Memory and Meditation

I want to address one additional area as it relates to meditation, because I believe that many people have been derailed by it. Some Christian leaders have equated Bible memorization with meditation, but the emphasis in Scripture is always on meditation. Scripture never commands us to memorize the Word of God. Many may argue that Psalm 119:11 commands us to memorize the Word. The verse actually says, "Thy word have I hid in mine heart." The actual word *hid* literally means to *treasure* God's Word in your heart. I believe that this is talking about meditation. Memory is for the head, but needs to go one step further to meditation. Meditation affects the heart.

I recently talked with a boy who was quoting some verses to me to finish up requirements for a teen Bible study. After he quoted a verse, I asked him what the verse meant. He replied, "I don't know. I just memorize it." Whoa! I realized I had gotten the cart before the horse. I was requiring this kid to recite verses but not to personalize truth. Do not get me wrong—I am not against Bible memorization. I just do not want to see us miss the boat on what is important to God.

Do not become discouraged by your lack of ability to memorize quickly. Concentrate on internalizing the truth of the passage. You will find that if you meditate on Bible verses day and night, you will end up memorizing them without much effort. The goal is to let the truth embed itself in your heart and make a permanent home.

Meditation, not memory, is the goal. Perhaps I can illustrate it this way.

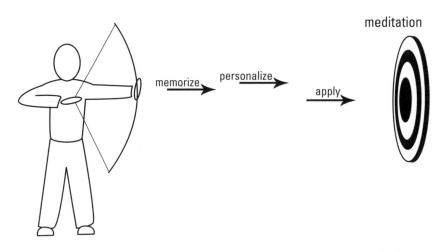

In other words, there are many ways to meditate on the Word of God. Bible memorization is certainly one of those ways that will aid you in the meditation process.

Now we need to look at how to make your meditation passage something that you can regularly think on throughout the day. If Scripture commands us to meditate day and night, I believe you should have those truths "on your person" at all times. Don't leave home without them. I mentioned earlier the need to have one truth, verse, or principle from your daily reading. You need to examine your lifestyle and figure out a way you can be reminded regularly of this truth—call it a Meditation Reminder. Find a Meditation Reminder that works for you. Two examples are:

- *Post-It notes in visible spots*

- *A 3 X 5 card*

Seeing the World Through God's Eyes

Once you begin to learn about God through His Word, you will begin to see more and more of God in the world. After learning how God has created everything for His glory, you will see the world through different eyes. Once you internalize truths, you will find it more and more natural to worship God as you walk through life. Every maternity ward you visit should remind you that babies are "fearfully and wonderfully made." Every snowstorm should be a chance to gaze at the wonder of a Creator God. When I visited the aquarium in our city recently, I marveled at how God, the Designer, fashioned each sea creature so uniquely and distinctly. When I drive to work, I ponder the creation I see around me. If I happen upon an accident, I muse over the protection of God, the grace of God. My mind can even begin meditating on death and how prepared I am for it. As I look through my e-mail, my mind ponders how to minister to the people to whom I need to reply. As I go to lunch, I meditate on the provision of God. When I am tempted, I think about my enemy Satan and how God has achieved the victory over him. When I drive home from work, I can meditate on the many gifts that God has given me—including a wonderful family. As I pillow my head at night, I can reflect on the works of God throughout the day.

This is a lifestyle of meditation. It is thinking through life with a God-focused lens. It is beholding the glory of the Lord in all of life. Ranew describes this when he describes meditation as having two parts:

1. *Things spiritual and heavenly,*

2. *Things, though not in themselves spiritual, yet in a spiritual manner looked upon.*[20]

I am describing the latter. David exhibited this lifestyle when he thought upon the growing of the grass, the singing of the birds, and the way of ships in the sea. Should we not also ponder the character and works of our great God?

I would be remiss if I did not mention the enemies of meditation. By far the greatest distraction is going to be a wandering or preoccupied mind. The Psalmist struggled with this—in Psalm 119:113 he said he hated "vain thoughts." Ranew says, "God complains of men when bodies are brought, and hearts are left out: well may He complain, if we go about meditation, mind, a thought exercise, if we let the mind and thoughts be sent abroad and not called home."[21] You will have to work hard to keep your mind from wandering. Ranew says later, "It is extremely against the grain of a natural heart, to be broken off from its customary wildness, wanderings, and rangings of thoughts; to cage up itself and become tame, and tuned to serious musings and thinkings heavenward."[22] Ranew also adds, "The mind is a spring always running in thinkings, a wheel always turning, a forge always framing, a wing ever moving; it is the most active, busy, nimble thing in all the world, therefore hath the greatest need to be well looked into."[23]

Remember, meditation is hard work. It is the most focused thought that a human being can have.

If meditation has not been a regular part of your daily diet, do not expect to become an expert meditator overnight. It will take time to re-train your mind to meditate on the Word of God, as opposed to the worries of this world. Make this truth the most valuable thing you take away from this book. Internalize the truth and practice it. The longer I gaze on Him throughout the day, the closer friend He becomes to me. "Meditation is of that happy influence, it makes the mind wise, the affections warm, the soul fat and flourishing, and the conversation greatly fruitful."[24]

Jesus, I am resting, resting
In the joy of what Thou art;
I am finding out the greatness
Of Thy loving heart.
Thou hast bid me gaze upon Thee,
And Thy beauty fills my soul,
For by Thy transforming power,
Thou hast made me whole.

—Jean Sophia Pigott, 1876

8

The Life That Touches Lives

In *Alone with God*, I have attempted to challenge you to engage in a dynamic daily walk with God. When you spend much time gazing upon God in the Word, He will change you to look like Him. Believers who look like Christ have a life message that impacts generations. I named my third son, Paton, after missionary John G. Paton, missionary to the New Hebrides Islands. John Paton was one of the greatest missionaries ever to live. When he came to the islands, the natives were given over to cannibalism, infanticide, and widow sacrifice. His life was constantly threatened, but he pursued his goal of delivering the gospel to the people. During his missionary tenure, he saw the entire island of Anniwa turn to Christ. Almost one hundred years after his death, his impact is still evident on the island. But what shaped Paton's life to make him the man that he was? Perhaps there was no human influence upon his life like that of his own father, James. In John Paton's autobiography, he gives us some pictures of this unknown man who had a worldwide impact.

His dad was committed to family worship, and at the age of seventeen, he convinced his mother, John Paton's grandmother, that family worship should not be held just on the Sabbath but every day. So they began morning and evening devotions which Paton later writes, he "practiced probably without one single avoidable omission till he lay on his death-bed at seventy-seven years of age . . . None of us can remember that any day passed unhallowed thus; no hurry for market, no rush to business, no arrival of friends or guests, no trouble or sorrow, no joy or excitement, ever prevented at least our kneeling around the family altar, while the High Priest led our prayers to God, and offered himself and his children there."[1]

He was committed to public worship. Regarding his dedication, he only missed church three times in forty years. Their Reformed Presbyterian Church was located four miles from their home and he was hindered "once by snow, so deep that he was baffled and had to return; once by ice on the road, so dangerous that he was forced to crawl back up the Roucan Brae on his hands and knees, after having descended it so far with many falls; and once by the terrible outbreak of cholera at Dumfries."[2] He had such a reputation for being faithful to the house of God that the farmers and villagers sent a message to his wife during the cholera outbreak urging her to restrain him from attending. On their way to church, they would listen in to the conversations the adults would have on the way. Paton says, "I have to bear my testimony that religion was presented with a great deal of intellectual freshness, and that it did not repel us, but kindled our spiritual interest . . . That, perhaps, makes all the difference betwixt talk that attracts and talk that drives away."[3] The lives of these saints made a profound impact on the young Paton.

He was devoted to spending time alone with God. Paton describes their home as a modest cottage. One end was the kitchen, dining room, beds, and parlor and the other end was his father's workshop where he made stockings. The mid-room was a very small room between the two that had room for a bed, a small table, and a chair. Paton called it the "sanctuary of that cottage home." Paton describes his father's devotional life this way,

"Thither daily, and oftentimes a day, generally after each meal, we saw our father retire, and 'shut to the door'; and we children got to understand by a sort of spiritual instinct (for the thing was too sacred to be talked about) that prayers were being poured out there for us, as of old by the High Priest within the veil in the Most Holy Place. We occasionally heard the pathetic echoes of a trembling voice pleading as if for life, and we learned to slip out and in past

that door on tiptoe, not to disturb the holy colloquy. The outside world might not know, but we knew, whence came that happy light as of a new-born smile that always was dawning on my father's face: it was a reflection from the Divine Presence, in the consciousness of which he lived. Never, in temple or cathedral, on mountain or in glen, can I hope to feel that the Lord God is more near, more visibly walking and talking with men, than under that humble cottage roof of thatch and oaken wattles. Though everything else in religion were by some unthinkable catastrophe to be swept out of memory, or blotted from my understanding, my soul would wander back to those early scenes, and shut itself up once again in that Sanctuary Closet, and, hearing still the echoes of those cries to God, would hurl back all doubt with the victorious appeal, 'He walked with God, why may not I?' "[4]

Paton's father had a burden for the lost. Paton describes how that one night during family worship, the worst woman in the village, given to a life of immorality, listened under their window as his father prayed for sinners to be converted. She later said, "I felt that I was a burden on that good man's heart, and I knew that God would not disappoint him. That thought kept me out of Hell, and at last led me to the only Saviour."[5] The passion that his father had for souls impacted young John. He writes,

"How much my father's prayers at this time impressed me I can never explain, nor could any stranger understand. When, on his knees and all of us kneeling around him in Family Worship, he poured out his whole soul with tears for the conversion of the Heathen world to the service of Jesus, and for every personal and domestic need, we all felt as if in the presence of the living Savior, and learned to know and love him as our Divine friend. As we rose from our knees I used to look at the light on my father's face, and wish I were like him in spirit—hoping that, in answer to his prayers, I might be privileged and prepared to carry the blessed Gospel to some portion of the Heathen World."[6]

Is it any wonder that the boy who came out of that home made a lasting impact upon the world? His father's relationship with God gave Paton a pattern and passion to follow. Once Paton set his eyes on the foreign field, nothing could turn him back. Regarded as foolish for going to cannibalistic islands, one old man said, "The cannibals! You will be eaten by cannibals!" John replied, "Mr. Dixon, you are advanced in years now and your own prospect is soon to be laid in the grave, there to be eaten by worms. I confess to you that if I can but live and die serving and honoring the Lord Jesus, it will make no difference to me whether my body is eaten by cannibals or by worms."[7] Paton impacted the world because his dad's life impacted him.

In college, I regularly heard from the pulpit, "A message prepared in the mind reaches minds, a message prepared in the heart reaches hearts, but a message prepared in the life reaches lives." Paul exhorted Timothy to not just go through the motions of religion, but live a life that was worthy of imitation. 1 Timothy 4:12b says, "Be thou an example of the believers, in word, in conversation, in charity, in spirit, in faith, in purity."

In *Alone with God*, my passion has been to encourage you to have a dynamic relationship with God. It is my prayer that you will fellowship with God and enjoy His presence. When the Word of Christ dwells in you richly, your life will touch the lives of countless others.

Appendix

Daily Journal Time Schedules

The actual time you spend is approximately twenty or thirty minutes, divided into eight segments. I have mapped out below how I divide the time based on a twenty- or thirty-minute plan. In the beginning, it may be helpful for you to jot down how much time you spend on each step until you get into a pattern. Keep in mind that this is only a suggested time frame. Feel free to adapt it to fit your needs.

30-Minute Plan

1. Preparation-2 minutes
2. Confession-1 minute
3. Revelation-10 minutes
4. Adoration-4 minutes
5. Transformation-4 minutes
6. Communication-4 minutes
7. & 8. Meditation and Application-5 minutes

20-Minute Plan

1. Preparation-1 minute
2. Confession-1 minute
3. Revelation-8 minutes
4. Adoration-2 minutes
5. Transformation-3 minutes
6. Communication-3 minutes
7. & 8. Meditation and Application-2 minutes

Devotional Plan   **Sample**

Preparation

Prayer ◆ Song ◆ Reading of a Christian book

My Plan Today:

(This area is to be filled in during the planning time.)

Confession

- Confession of known sin

My Plan Today:

Search Me, O God

Revelation

- Reading to know God through one Bible passage

My Plan Today:

(This area is to be filled in during the planning time.)

Adoration

- Prayer and songs of praise
- Prayer and songs of thanksgiving
- Praying the names of God

My Plan Today:

(This area is to be filled in during the planning time.)

Transformation

- Interactive reading and prayer of one chapter from Psalms or Proverbs

My Plan Today:

(This area is to be filled in during the planning time.)

Communication

- Prayer for personal needs
- Prayer for needs of others
- Prayer of casting cares upon the Lord
- Prayer of claiming a promise from God

My Plan Today:

(This area is to be filled in during the planning time.)

Devotional Journal   **Sample**

Meditation

What did God show me about Himself?

(This area is to be filled in after you complete the first six steps.)

What verse or truth from my two Bible readings will I meditate on day and night?

(This area is to be filled in after you complete the first six steps.)

Application

What did God, through His Word, tell me to do?

(This area is to be filled in after you complete the first six steps.)

Other Thoughts

(This area is to be filled in after you complete the first six steps.)

Song Index

These pages are provided for you to build your own list of songs for your devotions. Most hymnals and songbooks have indexes of songs listed by topic which can be a great help. If you like to use recorded music during your devotions, pull out your music collection and catalog your favorite songs into the appropriate category. The first three categories are directly from the Devotional Planner. I have also added an "Other" category, since you may want to close out your devotional time with a favorite song.

Preparation Songs

_____   _____

_____   _____

_____   _____

_____   _____

_____   _____

_____   _____

_____   _____

Confession Songs

_____   _____

_____   _____

_____   _____

_____   _____

_____   _____

_____   _____

_____   _____

Adoration Songs—Songs of Praise and Thanksgiving

_____   _____

_____   _____

_____   _____

_____   _____

_____   _____

_____   _____

_____   _____

Other Songs

_____   _____

_____   _____

_____   _____

_____   _____

_____   _____

_____   _____

Confession Step Helps

Sins Identified in Scripture

Sins of the Family

1. Adultery
2. Divorce
3. Variance
4. Disobedience to parents
5. Neglect of discipline
6. Dishonor
7. Lack of communication
8. Neglect of family time
9. Neglect of family prayer and devotions
10. Burdensome debt
11. Rebellion in children
12. Husbands not loving their wives
13. Wives not submitting to their husbands
14. Abuse and incest
15. Fighting and bickering
16. Debate and strife
17. Nagging
18. Unwillingness to forgive
19. Complaining
20. Unfaithfulness to church
21. Failure to make reconciliation
22. Failure to witness to your relatives
23. Lack of love

Sins of the Church

1. Failure to pray
2. Whispering/backbiting/ evil speaking
3. Failure to share the gospel
4. False accusations
5. Worldliness
6. Sedition
7. Heresy
8. Laziness of church workers
9. Rebellion against pastoral leadership
10. Failure to be salt in a corrupt world
11. Lukewarmness and carnality
12. Compromise with false doctrine
13. Failure to support missionaries
14. Gossip against church members
15. Powerlessness among believers
16. Neglect of the Holy Spirit's ministry
17. Unbelief of leaders to go forward in faith
18. Immorality of church members
19. Division among believers
20. Participation in wrong music, TV, and movies
21. Lack of love among believers
22. Neglect of attendance to house of worship
23. Failure to respond after hearing the Word

Personal Sins

1. Wickedness/ unrighteousness
2. Corrupt communication
3. Reprobate thoughts / lasciviousness/evil thoughts
4. Maliciousness
5. Pride/heady/high-mindedness/ boasters
6. Dishonesty/deceit/lying

7. Fornication
8. Murder
9. Witchcraft
10. Lack of mercy/implacableness
11. Strife/reviling
12. Drunkenness
13. Reveling
14. Railing
15. Extortion
16. Blasphemy
17. Foolishness
18. Disorderly conduct/brawler
19. Bitterness
20. Hatred
21. Envy/an evil eye
22. Jealousy
23. Stealing
24. Cursing/Profanity
25. Lust
26. Immorality
27. Idolatry
28. Indulgence
29. Unbelief
30. Lack of self-discipline
31. Unnatural, vile affections/homosexuality
32. Impure thoughts
33. Neglect of the Bible
34. Worldliness
35. Foolish talking/jesting
36. Evil concupiscence
37. Fierceness
38. Covetousness
39. Selfishness
40. Gossip
41. Wrath/anger
42. Greed
43. Criticism
44. Complaining
45. Disrespect
46. Unthankfulness
47. Failure to tithe
48. Laziness
49. Rebellion

Sins of the Nation

1. Abortion
2. Removal of prayer from the public square
3. Homosexuality/unnatural, vile affections
4. Truce/covenant breaking
5. Immorality
6. Loving pleasure more than loving God
7. Materialism
8. Haters of God
9. Men stealers (slavery)
10. Murder
11. Traitors
12. Drug abuse
13. Legalized gambling (lottery)
14. Failure to honor the Lord's Day
15. Unbelief in the universities
16. Corruption in government
17. Corruption in entertainment
18. Excessive governmental debt
19. Persecution of Christians

Adapted from *How To Pray Thirty Minutes A Day* by Steve Pettit (used with permission)

Penitential Passages in Scripture

Psalm 32:1–8 *"Blessed is he whose transgression is forgiven, whose sin is covered. Blessed is the man unto whom the Lord imputeth not iniquity, and in whose spirit there is no guile. When I kept silence, my bones waxed old through my roaring all the day long. For day and night thy hand was heavy upon me: my moisture is turned into the drought of summer. Selah. I acknowledged my sin unto thee, and mine iniquity have I not hid. I said, I will confess my transgressions unto the Lord; and thou forgavest the iniquity of my sin. Selah. For this shall every one that is godly pray unto thee in a time when thou mayest be found: surely in the floods of great waters they shall not come nigh unto him. Thou art my hiding place; thou shalt preserve me from trouble; thou shalt compass me about with songs of deliverance. Selah. I will instruct thee and teach thee in the way which thou shalt go: I will guide thee with mine eye."*

Psalm 51:1–17 *"Have mercy upon me, O God, according to thy lovingkindness: according unto the multitude of thy tender mercies blot out my transgressions. Wash me throughly from mine iniquity, and cleanse me from my sin. For I acknowledge my transgressions: and my sin is ever before me. Against thee, thee only, have I sinned, and done this evil in thy sight: that thou mightest be justified when thou speakest, and be clear when thou judgest. Behold, I was shapen in iniquity; and in sin did my mother conceive me. Behold, thou desirest truth in the inward parts: and in the hidden part thou shalt make me to know wisdom. Purge me with hyssop, and I shall be clean: wash me, and I shall be whiter than snow. Make me to hear joy and gladness; that the bones which thou hast broken may rejoice. Hide thy face from my sins, and blot out all mine iniquities. Create in me a clean heart, O God; and renew a right spirit within me. Cast me not away from thy presence; and take not thy holy spirit from me. Restore unto me the joy of thy salvation; and uphold me with thy free spirit. Then will I teach transgressors thy ways; and sinners shall be converted unto thee. Deliver me from bloodguiltiness, O God, thou God of my salvation: and my tongue shall sing aloud of thy righteousness. O Lord, open thou my lips; and my mouth shall shew forth thy praise. For thou desirest not sacrifice; else would I give it: thou delightest not in burnt offering. The sacrifices of God are a broken spirit: a broken and a contrite heart, O God, thou wilt not despise."*

Other Penitential Psalms: Psalms 6, 38, 51, 102, 130, and 142

Revelation Step Reading Guide

Easy	Moderate	Difficult
*Genesis	Deuteronomy	Leviticus
Exodus	1 Chronicles	Numbers
Joshua	2 Chronicles	Isaiah
Judges	Job	Jeremiah
Ruth	Song of Solomon	Lamentations
1 Samuel	Romans	Ezekiel
2 Samuel	Galatians	Hosea
1 Kings	Colossians	Joel
2 Kings	Titus	Amos
Ezra	Philemon	Obadiah
Nehemiah	Hebrews	Micah
Esther	Jude	Nahum
Ecclesiastes		Habakkuk
Daniel		Zephaniah
Jonah		Haggai
Matthew		Zechariah
Mark		Malachi
Luke		Revelation
*John		
*Acts		
1 Corinthians		
2 Corinthians		
Ephesians		
Philippians		
1 Thessalonians		
2 Thessalonians		
1 Timothy		
2 Timothy		
*James		
1 Peter		
2 Peter		
*1 John		
2 John		
3 John		

Psalms and Proverbs have been omitted because they are the texts for the Transformation Step.

* These books will be the best books to start with if you have never had a Bible reading plan.

Adoration Step Helps

*Names of God
Identified in Scripture*

Names of God the Father

1. A Forgiving God
2. A Fortress of Salvation
3. A Glorious Crown
4. A Jealous and Avenging God
5. A Master in Heaven
6. A Refuge for His People
7. A Refuge for the Poor
8. A Sanctuary
9. A Shade from the Heat
10. A Shelter from the Storm
11. A Source of Strength
12. A Stronghold in Times of Trouble
13. An Ever-present Help in Trouble
14. Architect and Builder
15. Commander of the Lord's Army
16. Creator of Heaven and Earth
17. Defender of Widows
18. Eternal King
19. Father
20. Father of Compassion
21. Father of Our Spirits
22. Father to the fatherless
23. God
24. God Almighty (El Sabbaoth)
25. God Almighty (El Shaddai)
26. God and Father of Our Lord Jesus Christ
27. God Most High
28. God My Maker
29. God My Rock
30. God My Savior
31. God My Stronghold
32. God of Abraham, Isaac, and Jacob
33. God of All Comfort
34. God of Glory
35. God of Gods
36. God of Grace
37. God of Hope
38. God of Love
39. God of Peace
40. God of Retribution
41. God of the Living
42. God of the Spirits of All Mankind
43. God of Truth
44. God Our Father
45. God Our Strength
46. God over All the Kingdoms of the Earth
47. God Who Avenges Me
48. God Who Gives Endurance and Encouragement
49. Great and Awesome God
50. He Who Blots Out Your Transgressions
51. He Who Comforts You
52. He Who Forms the Hearts of All
53. He Who Is Able to Do Immeasurably More Than All We Ask or Imagine
54. He Who Is Able to Keep You From Falling
55. He Who is Ready to Judge the Living and the Dead
56. He Who raised Christ from the Dead
57. He Who Reveals His Thoughts to Man
58. Helper of the Fatherless
59. Holy Father

60. Holy One
61. Holy One Among You
62. I AM
63. I AM WHO I AM
64. Jealous
65. Judge of All the Earth
66. King of Glory
67. King of Heaven
68. Living and True God
69. Lord (Adonai)
70. Lord Almighty
71. Lord God Almighty
72. Lord (Yahweh)
73. Lord Most High
74. Lord My Banner
75. Lord My Rock
76. Lord of All the Earth
77. Lord of Heaven and Earth
78. Lord Our God
79. Lord Our Maker
80. Lord Our Shield
81. Lord Who Heals You
82. Lord Who Is There
83. Lord Who Makes You Holy
84. Lord Will Provide
85. Love
86. Maker of All Things
87. Maker of Heaven and Earth
88. Most High
89. My Advocate
90. My Comforter in sorrow
91. My Confidence
92. My Help
93. My Helper
94. My Hiding Place
95. My Hope
96. My Light
97. My Mighty Rock
98. My Refuge in the Day of Disaster
99. My Refuge In Times of Trouble
100. My Song
101. My Strong Deliverer
102. My Support
103. One to Be Feared
104. Only Wise God
105. Our Dwelling Place
106. Our Judge
107. Our Lawgiver
108. Our Leader
109. Our Mighty One
110. Our Redeemer
111. Our Refuge and Strength
112. Righteous Father
113. Righteous Judge
114. Rock of Our Salvation
115. Shepherd
116. Sovereign Lord
117. The Almighty
118. The Compassionate and Gracious God
119. The Consuming Fire
120. The Eternal God
121. The Everlasting God
122. The Exalted God
123. The Faithful God
124. The Gardener (Husbandman)
125. The Glorious Father
126. The Glory of Israel
127. The God Who Saved Me
128. The God Who Sees Me
129. The Great King Above All Gods
130. The Just and Almighty One
131. The Living Father
132. The Majestic Glory
133. The Majesty of Heaven
134. The One Who Sustains Me
135. The Only God
136. The Potter
137. The Rock in Whom I Take Refuge

138. The Spring of Living Water
139. The Strength of My Heart
140. The True God
141. You Who Hear Prayer
142. You Who Judge Righteously and Test the Heart and Mind
143. You Who Keep Your Covenant of Love with Your Servants
144. You Who Love the People
145. Your Glory
146. Your Praise
147. Your Very Great Reward

Names of Jesus

1. A Banner for the Peoples
2. A Nazarene
3. All
4. Alpha and Omega
5. Ancient of Days
6. Anointed One
7. Apostle and High Priest
8. Author and Perfecter of Our Faith
9. Author of Life
10. Author of Salvation
11. Blessed and Only Ruler
12. Branch of the Lord
13. Bread of God
14. Bread of Life
15. Bridegroom
16. Chief Cornerstone
17. Chief Shepherd
18. Chosen and Precious
19. Cornerstone
20. Christ Jesus My Lord
21. Christ Jesus Our Hope
22. Christ of God
23. Consolation of Israel
24. Covenant of the People
25. Crown of Splendor
26. Eternal Life
27. Faithful and True
28. First to Rise from the Dead
29. Firstborn from Among the Dead
30. Firstborn over All Creation
31. Firstfruits of Those That Have Fallen Asleep
32. Fragrant Offering and Sacrifice to God
33. Friend of Tax Collectors and Sinners
34. God of All the Earth
35. God over All
36. God's Son
37. Great High Priest
38. Great Light
39. Great Shepherd of the Sheep
40. Guarantee of a Better Covenant
41. He Who Comes down from Heaven and Gives Life to the World
42. He Who Died and Came to Life Again
43. He Who Loves Us and Has Freed Us from our Sins
44. He Who Searches Hearts and Minds
45. Head of Every Man
46. Head of the Body (the Church)
47. Head over Every Power and Authority
48. Heir of All Things
49. His One and Only Son
50. Holy and Righteous One
51. Holy One of God
52. Holy Servant Jesus
53. Hope of Israel
54. Horn of Salvation
55. Image of the Invisible God
56. Immanuel (God With Us)
57. Indescribable Gift

58. Jesus
59. Jesus Christ
60. Jesus Christ Our Lord
61. Jesus Christ Our Savior
62. Jesus of Nazareth
63. Judge of the Living and the Dead
64. King Of Kings
65. King of the Ages
66. Lamb of God
67. Light for Revelation to the Gentiles
68. Light of Life
69. Light of Men
70. Light of the World
71. Living Bread That Came Down from Heaven
72. Lord and Savior Jesus Christ
73. Lord (Kurios)
74. Lord Of Lords
75. Lord of Peace
76. Lord of the Harvest
77. Lord of the Sabbath
78. Man Accredited by God
79. Man of Sorrows
80. Master
81. Mediator of a New Covenant
82. Merciful and Faithful High Priest
83. Messenger of the Covenant
84. Messiah
85. Morning Star
86. My Friend
87. My Intercessor
88. One Who Makes Men Holy
89. One Who Speaks to the Father in Our Defense
90. One Who Will Arise to Rule over the Nations
91. Our Glorious Lord Jesus Christ
92. Our Only Sovereign and Lord
93. Our Passover Lamb
94. Our Peace
95. Our Righteousness, Holiness, and Redemption
96. Physician
97. Prince and Savior
98. Prince of Peace
99. Prince of Princes
100. Prince of the Hosts
101. Rabbi/Rabboni (Teacher)
102. Ransom for All Men
103. Refiner and Purifier
104. Resurrection
105. Righteous Judge
106. Righteous Man
107. Righteous One
108. Rock Eternal (Rock of Ages)
109. Ruler of God's Creation
110. Ruler of the Kings of the Earth
111. Savior of the World
112. Second Man
113. Shepherd and Overseer of Your Souls
114. Son of Man
115. Son of the Blessed One
116. Son of the Living One
117. Son of the Most High God
118. Source of Eternal Salvation
119. Sure Foundation
120. Teacher
121. The Amen
122. The Atoning Sacrifice for Our Sins
123. The Beginning and the End
124. The Bright and Morning Star
125. The Exact Representation of His Being
126. The First and the Last
127. The Gate (Door)
128. The Head
129. The Last Adam

130. The Life
131. The Living One
132. The Living Stone
133. The Lord our Righteousness
134. The Man from Heaven
135. The Man Jesus Christ
136. The Most Holy
137. The One and Only
138. The Only God our Savior
139. The Radiance of God's Glory
140. The Rising of the Sun (Day-spring)
141. The Stone the Builders Rejected
142. The Testimony Given in Its Proper Time
143. The True Light
144. The True Vine
145. The Truth
146. The Way
147. The Word (Logos)
148. True Bread from Heaven
149. Wisdom from God
150. Witness to the Peoples
151. Wonderful Counselor
152. Word of God
153. Word of Life
154. Your Life
155. Your Salvation

Names of the Holy Spirit
1. A Deposit (Earnest)
2. Another Counselor
3. Breath of the Almighty
4. Holy One
5. Holy Spirit of God
6. Seal
7. Spirit of Christ
8. Spirit of Counsel and of Power
9. Spirit of Faith
10. Spirit of Fire

11. Spirit of Glory
12. Spirit of God
13. Spirit of Grace and Supplication
14. Spirit of His Son
15. Spirit of Holiness
16. Spirit of Jesus Christ
17. Spirit of Judgement
18. Spirit of Justice
19. Spirit of Knowledge and of the Fear of the Lord
20. Spirit of Life
21. Spirit of our God
22. Spirit of Sonship (Adoption)
23. Spirit of the Living God
24. Spirit of the Lord
25. Spirit of the Sovereign Lord
26. Spirit of Truth
27. Spirit of Wisdom and of Understanding
28. Spirit of Wisdom and Revelation
29. The Gift
30. The Promised Holy Spirit
31. Voice of the Almighty
32. Voice of the Lord

Adapted from *How to Pray Thirty Minutes A Day* by Steve Pettit (used with permission)

128

Transformation Step Reading Guide

Psalms

Psalm 1	Psalm 39	Psalm 77	Psalm 115
Psalm 2	Psalm 40	Psalm 78	Psalm 116
Psalm 3	Psalm 41	Psalm 79	Psalm 117
Psalm 4	Psalm 42	Psalm 80	Psalm 118
*Psalm 5	Psalm 43	Psalm 81	Psalm 119
Psalm 6	Psalm 44	Psalm 82	Psalm 120
Psalm 7	Psalm 45	Psalm 83	Psalm 121
Psalm 8	Psalm 46	Psalm 84	Psalm 122
Psalm 9	Psalm 47	Psalm 85	Psalm 123
Psalm 10	Psalm 48	Psalm 86	Psalm 124
*Psalm 11	Psalm 49	Psalm 87	Psalm 125
Psalm 12	Psalm 50	Psalm 88	Psalm 126
Psalm 13	Psalm 51	Psalm 89	Psalm 127
Psalm 14	Psalm 52	Psalm 90	Psalm 128
Psalm 15	Psalm 53	Psalm 91	Psalm 129
Psalm 16	Psalm 54	Psalm 92	Psalm 130
*Psalm 17	*Psalm 55	Psalm 93	Psalm 131
Psalm 18	Psalm 56	Psalm 94	Psalm 132
Psalm 19	Psalm 57	Psalm 95	Psalm 133
Psalm 20	Psalm 58	Psalm 96	Psalm 134
Psalm 21	*Psalm 59	Psalm 97	Psalm 135
Psalm 22	Psalm 60	Psalm 98	Psalm 136
Psalm 23	Psalm 61	Psalm 99	*Psalm 137
Psalm 24	Psalm 62	Psalm 100	Psalm 138
Psalm 25	Psalm 63	Psalm 101	Psalm 139
Psalm 26	Psalm 64	Psalm 102	*Psalm 140
Psalm 27	Psalm 65	Psalm 103	Psalm 141
Psalm 28	Psalm 66	Psalm 104	Psalm 142
Psalm 29	Psalm 67	Psalm 105	Psalm 143
Psalm 30	Psalm 68	Psalm 106	Psalm 144
Psalm 31	*Psalm 69	Psalm 107	Psalm 145
Psalm 32	Psalm 70	Psalm 108	Psalm 146
Psalm 33	Psalm 71	*Psalm 109	Psalm 147
Psalm 34	Psalm 72	Psalm 110	Psalm 148
*Psalm 35	Psalm 73	Psalm 111	Psalm 149
Psalm 36	Psalm 74	Psalm 112	Psalm 150
Psalm 37	Psalm 75	Psalm 113	
Psalm 38	Psalm 76	Psalm 114	

*Indicates Imprecatory Psalm

Proverbs

Proverbs 1
Proverbs 2
Proverbs 3
Proverbs 4
Proverbs 5
Proverbs 6
Proverbs 7
Proverbs 8
Proverbs 9
Proverbs 10
Proverbs 11
Proverbs 12
Proverbs 13
Proverbs 14
Proverbs 15

Proverbs 16
Proverbs 17
Proverbs 18
Proverbs 19
Proverbs 20
Proverbs 21
Proverbs 22
Proverbs 23
Proverbs 24
Proverbs 25
Proverbs 26
Proverbs 27
Proverbs 28
Proverbs 29
Proverbs 30
Proverbs 31

*Additional
passages:*

Communication Step Prayer Journal

My Every-Day Prayer List

Once-a-Week Prayer List

Sunday

Week of : _____

Monday

Tuesday

Wednesday

Thursday

Friday

Saturday

Communication Step Bible Promises

Numbers 23:19—God is not a man, that he should lie; neither the son of man, that he should repent: hath he said, and shall he not do it? or hath he spoken, and shall he not make it good?

2 Peter 1:4—Whereby are given unto us exceeding great and precious promises: that by these ye might be partakers of the divine nature, having escaped the corruption that is in the world through lust.

Anger

Proverbs 15:1a—A soft answer turneth away wrath.

Proverbs 25:21–22—If thine enemy be hungry, give him bread to eat; and if he be thirsty, give him water to drink: For thou shalt heap coals of fire upon his head, and the Lord shall reward thee.

Children

Ephesians 6:1–3—Children, obey your parents in the Lord: for this is right. Honour thy father and mother; (which is the first commandment with promise;) That it may be well with thee, and thou mayest live long on the earth.

Comfort

Psalm 46:1–3—God is our refuge and strength, a very present help in trouble. Therefore will not we fear, though the earth be removed, and though the mountains be carried into the midst of the sea; Though the waters thereof roar and be troubled, though the mountains shake with the swelling thereof. Selah.

Psalm 55:22—Cast thy burden upon the Lord, and he shall sustain thee: he shall never suffer the righteous to be moved.

Matthew 11:28—Come unto me, all ye that labour and are heavy laden, and I will give you rest.

Confession and Forgiveness

1 John 1:9—If we confess our sins, he is faithful and just to forgive us our sins, and to cleanse us from all unrighteousness.

Psalm 103:12—As far as the east is from the west, so far hath he removed our transgressions from us.

Jeremiah 31:34b—For I will forgive their iniquity, and I will remember their sin no more.

Matthew 6:14—For if ye forgive men their trespasses, your heavenly Father will also forgive you.

Contentment

Hebrews 13:5—Let your conversation be without covetousness; and be content with such things as ye have: for he hath said, I will never leave thee, nor forsake thee.

Correction

Proverbs 3:12a—For whom the Lord loveth he correcteth.

Courage

Isaiah 40:29—He giveth power to the faint; and to them that have no might he increaseth strength.

Philippians 4:13—I can do all things through Christ which strengtheneth me.

Death

Psalm 23:4—Yea, though I walk through the valley of the shadow of death, I will fear no evil: for thou art with me; thy rod and thy staff they comfort me.

Enemies

Proverbs 16:7—When a man's ways please the Lord, he maketh even his enemies to be at peace with him.

Hebrew 13:6—So that we may boldly say, The Lord is my helper, and I will not fear what man shall do unto me.

Failure

Psalm 37:23–24—The steps of a good man are ordered by the Lord: and he delighteth in his way. Though he fall, he shall not be utterly cast down: for the Lord upholdeth him with His hand.

Faith

James 1:5–6—If any of you lack wisdom, let him ask of God, that giveth to all men liberally, and upbraideth not; and it shall be given him. But let him ask in faith, nothing wavering. For he that wavereth is like a wave of the sea driven with the wind and tossed.

Faithfulness of God

Psalm 9:10—And they that know thy name will put their trust in thee: for thou, Lord, hast not forsaken them that seek thee.

Fear

Proverbs 1:33—But whoso hearkeneth unto me shall dwell safely, and shall be quiet from fear of evil.

2 Timothy 1:7—For God hath not given us the spirit of fear; but of power, and of love, and of a sound mind.

Proverbs 29:25—The fear of man bringeth a snare: but whoso putteth his trust in the Lord shall be safe.

Freedom from Sin
Romans 6:14a—For sin shall not have dominion over you.

Fruitfulness
John 15:5—I am the vine, ye are the branches: he that abideth in me, and I in him, the same bringeth forth much fruit: for without me ye can do nothing.

Giving
Psalm 41:1–2—Blessed is he that considereth the poor: the Lord will deliver him in time of trouble. The Lord will preserve him, and keep him alive; and he shall be blessed upon the earth: and thou wilt not deliver him unto the will of his enemies.

Proverbs 19:17—He that hath pity upon the poor lendeth unto the Lord; and that which he hath given will he pay him again.

Luke 6:38—Give, and it shall be given unto you; good measure, pressed down, and shaken together, and running over, shall men give into your bosom. For with the same measure that ye mete withal it shall be measured to you again.

Proverbs 28:27—He that giveth unto the poor shall not lack: but he that hideth his eyes shall have many a curse.

Growth in Grace
Psalm 138:8a—The Lord will perfect that which concerneth me.

Guidance
Proverbs 16:9—A man's heart deviseth his way: but the Lord directeth his steps.

Proverbs 3:5–6—Trust in the Lord with all thine heart; and lean not unto thine own understanding. In all thy ways acknowledge him, and he shall direct thy paths.

John 16:13—Howbeit when he, the Spirit of truth, is come, he will guide you into all truth: for he shall not speak of himself; but whatsoever he shall hear, that shall he speak: and he will shew you things to come.

Help in Trouble
Nahum 1:7—The Lord is good, a strong hold in the day of trouble; and he knoweth them that trust in him.

Psalm 42:11—Why art thou cast down, O my soul? and why art thou disquieted within me? hope thou in God: for I shall yet praise him, who is the health of my countenance, and my God.

Psalm 34:19—Many are the afflictions of the righteous: but the Lord delivereth him out of them all.

Psalm 18:2—The Lord is my rock, and my fortress, and my deliverer; my God, my strength, in whom I will trust; my buckler, and the horn of my salvation, and my high tower.

Honesty

Proverbs 12:19—The lip of truth shall be established for ever: but a lying tongue is but for a moment.

Hospitality

Acts 20:35b—It is more blessed to give than to receive.

Humility

Matthew 23:12—And whosoever shall exalt himself shall be abased; and he that shall humble himself shall be exalted.

James 4:6—But he giveth more grace. Wherefore he saith, God resisteth the proud, but giveth grace unto the humble.

Joy

Nehemiah 8:10c—For the joy of the Lord is your strength.

Long Life

Proverbs 3:1–2—My son, forget not my law; but let thine heart keep my commandments: For length of days, and long life, and peace, shall they add to thee.

Proverbs 10:27—The fear of the Lord prolongeth days: but the years of the wicked shall be shortened.

Love of God

1 John 4:10—Herein is love, not that we loved God, but that he loved us, and sent his Son to be the propitiation for our sins.

Jeremiah 31:3—The Lord hath appeared of old unto me, saying, Yea, I have loved thee with an everlasting love: therefore with lovingkindness have I drawn thee.

1 John 4:19—We love him, because he first loved us.

Romans 8:38–39—For I am persuaded, that neither death, nor life, nor angels, nor principalities, nor powers, nor things present, nor things to come, Nor height, nor depth, nor any other creature, shall be able to separate us from the love of God, which is in Christ Jesus our Lord.

Loving God

Proverbs 8:17—I love them that love me; and those that seek me early shall find me.

Psalm 37:4—Delight thyself also in the Lord; and he shall give thee the desires of thine heart.

1 Corinthians 2:9—But as it is written, Eye hath not seen, nor ear heard, neither have entered into the heart of man, the things which God hath prepared for them that love him.

Lust

1 John 2:16–17—For all that is in the world, the lust of the flesh, and the lust of the eyes, and the pride of life, is not of the Father, but is of the world. And the world passeth away, and the lust thereof: but he that doeth the will of God abideth for ever.

James 4:7–8a—Submit yourselves therefore to God. Resist the devil, and he will flee from you. Draw nigh to God, and he will draw nigh to you.

Meekness

Matthew 5:5—Blessed are the meek: for they shall inherit the earth.

Psalm 22:26—The meek shall eat and be satisfied: they shall praise the Lord that seek him: your heart shall live for ever.

Mercy

Psalm 103:17—But the mercy of the Lord is from everlasting to everlasting upon them that fear him, and his righteousness unto children's children.

Money

Proverbs 23:5a—For riches certainly make themselves wings; they fly away as an eagle toward heaven.

Proverbs 11:28—He that trusteth in his riches shall fall; but the righteous shall flourish as a branch.

Proverbs 28:20a—A faithful man shall abound with blessings.

Proverbs 13:7—There is that maketh himself rich, yet hath nothing: there is that maketh himself poor, yet hath great riches.

Obedience

Philippians 4:9—Those things, which ye have both learned, and received, and heard, and seen in me, do: and the God of peace shall be with you.

Romans 8:28—And we know that all things work together for good to them that love God, to them who are the called according to his purpose.

1 John 2:17—And the world passeth away, and the lust thereof: but he that doeth the will of God abideth for ever.

Patience

Galatians 6:9—And let us not be weary in well doing: for in due season we shall reap, if we faint not.

James 1:2–4—My brethren, count it all joy when ye fall into divers temptations; Knowing this, that the trying of your faith worketh patience. But let patience have her perfect work, that ye may be perfect and entire, wanting nothing.

Peace

Philippians 4:7—And the peace of God, which passeth all understanding, shall keep your hearts and minds through Christ Jesus.

John 16:33—These things I have spoken unto you, that in me ye might have peace. In the world ye shall have tribulation: but be of good cheer; I have overcome the world.

Prayer

Matthew 7:7–8—Ask, and it shall be given you; seek, and ye shall find; knock, and it shall be opened unto you; For every one that asketh receiveth; and he that seeketh findeth; and to him that knocketh it shall be opened.

Matthew 21:22—And all things, whatsoever ye shall ask in prayer, believing, ye shall receive.

James 5:16b—The effectual fervent prayer of a righteous man availeth much.

Matthew 6:6—But thou, when thou prayest, enter into thy closet, and when thou hast shut thy door, pray to thy Father which is in secret; and thy Father which seeth in secret shall reward thee openly.

Pride

Proverbs 16:18—Pride goeth before destruction, and an haughty spirit before a fall.

Mark 9:35—And he sat down, and called the twelve, and saith unto them, If any man desire to be first, the same shall be last of all, and servant of all.

Protection of God

Proverbs 1:33—But whoso hearkeneth unto me shall dwell safely, and shall be quiet from fear of evil.

Psalm 27:1—The Lord is my light and my salvation; whom shall I fear? the Lord is the strength of my life; of whom shall I be afraid?

Righteousness

Psalm 84:11—For the Lord God is a sun and shield: the Lord will give grace and glory: no good thing will he withhold from them that walk uprightly.

Matthew 6:33—But seek ye first the kingdom of God, and his righteousness; and all these things shall be added unto you.

Seeking God

Hebrews 11:6—But without faith it is impossible to please him: for he that cometh to God must believe that he is, and that he is a rewarder of them that diligently seek him.

Lamentations 3:25—The Lord is good unto them that wait for him, to the soul that seeketh him.

Jeremiah 29:13—And ye shall seek me, and find me, when ye shall search for me with all your heart.

Strength

Psalm 73:26—My flesh and my heart faileth: but God is the strength of my heart, and my portion for ever.

Success

Psalm 1:3—And he shall be like a tree planted by the rivers of water, that bringeth forth his fruit in his season; his leaf also shall not wither; and whatsoever he doeth shall prosper.

Joshua 1:8—This book of the law shall not depart out of thy mouth; but thou shalt meditate therein day and night, that thou mayest observe to do according to all that is written therein: for then thou shalt make thy way prosperous, and then thou shalt have good success.

Temptation

1 Corinthians 10:13—There hath no temptation taken you but such as is common to man: but God is faithful, who will not suffer you to be tempted above that ye are able; but will with the temptation also make a way to escape, that ye may be able to bear it.

Hebrews 4:15–16—For we have not an high priest which cannot be touched with the feeling of our infirmities; but was in all points tempted like as we are, yet without sin. Let us therefore come boldly unto the throne of grace, that we may obtain mercy, and find grace to help in time of need.

Trust

Psalm 37:5—Commit thy way unto the Lord; trust also in him; and he shall bring it to pass.

1 Peter 5:7—Casting all your care upon him; for he careth for you.

Waiting on God

Psalm 27:14—Wait on the Lord: be of good courage, and he shall strengthen thine heart: wait, I say, on the Lord.

Wisdom

James 1:5–6—If any of you lack wisdom, let him ask of God, that giveth to all men liberally, and upbraideth not; and it shall be given him. But let him ask in faith, nothing wavering. For he that wavereth is like a wave of the sea driven with the wind and tossed.

Proverbs 28:5—Evil men understand not judgment: but they that seek the Lord understand all things.

Word of God

Romans 1:16a—For I am not ashamed of the gospel of Christ: for it is the power of God unto salvation to every one that believeth.

Psalm 119:130 The entrance of thy words giveth light; it giveth understanding unto the simple.

Romans 10:17—So then faith cometh by hearing, and hearing by the word of God.

1 Peter 2:2—As newborn babes, desire the sincere milk of the word, that ye may grow thereby.

Psalm 119:105—Thy word is a lamp unto my feet, and a light unto my path.

Work

Proverbs 28:19—He that tilleth his land shall have plenty of bread: but he that followeth after vain persons shall have poverty enough.

Proverbs 10:4–5—He becometh poor that dealeth with a slack hand: but the hand of the diligent maketh rich. He that gathereth in summer is a wise son: but he that sleepeth in harvest is a son that causeth shame.

Proverbs 20:13—Love not sleep, lest thou come to poverty; open thine eyes, and thou shalt be satisfied with bread.

Worry

Philippians 4:6–7—Be careful for nothing; but in every thing by prayer and supplication with thanksgiving let your requests be made known unto God. And the peace of God, which passeth all understanding, shall keep your hearts and minds through Christ Jesus.

Philippians 4:19—But my God shall supply all your need according to his riches in glory by Christ Jesus.

How to Begin My Relationship with God

The Gospel

God's plan of salvation is simple and open to all. If you are unsure of your relationship with God, I encourage you to read the following Scriptures.

Realize that God loves you.

"For God so loved the world, that he gave his only begotten Son, that whosoever believeth in him should not perish, but have everlasting life." John 3:16

Realize that you are a sinner.

"For all have sinned, and come short of the glory of God." Romans 3:23

Realize that a price must be paid for your sin.

"For the wages of sin is death; but the gift of God is eternal life through Jesus Christ our Lord." Romans 6:23

Realize that good works cannot pay for your sin.

"For by grace are ye saved through faith; and that not of yourselves: it is the gift of God: Not of works, lest any man should boast." Ephesians 2:8–9

Realize that Jesus Christ died to pay the price for your sin.

"But God commendeth his love toward us, in that, while we were yet sinners, Christ died for us." Romans 5:8

Trust Him alone to save you.

"For whosoever shall call upon the name of the Lord shall be saved." Romans 10:13

If you have never put your full trust in Christ for salvation, I would encourage you to get saved right now. I have printed a sample prayer for you to follow if you would like to accept Christ. You are not saved because of this prayer, but because of your trust in Christ.

"Lord, I know that I have sinned and am separated from You. I cannot save myself. I believe that You love me and sent Your son Jesus to die on the cross to make a way of escape. I realize that trusting in my own good works or myself cannot get me to heaven, and I am willing to rely fully upon Jesus Christ's sacrificial death on the cross to pay my way to heaven. From this time on, I desire to look to Him for guidance and abundant life, as I desire to grow as a Christian. In Jesus' name, Amen."

Soul Nourishment First

A Booklet by George Mueller[1]
May 9, 1841

It has pleased the Lord to teach me a truth, the benefit of which I have not lost, for more than fourteen years. The point is this:

I saw more clearly than ever that the first great and primary business to which I ought to attend every day was, to have my soul happy in the Lord. The first thing to be concerned about was not how much I might serve the Lord, or how I might glorify the Lord; but how I might get my soul into a happy state, and how my inner man might be nourished. For I might seek to set the truth before the unconverted, I might seek to benefit believers, I might seek to relieve the distressed, I might in other ways seek to behave myself as it becomes a child of God in this world; and yet, not being happy in the Lord, and not being nourished and strengthened in my inner man day by day, all this might not be attended to in a right spirit.

Before this time my practice had been, at least for ten years previously, as an habitual thing, to give myself to prayer, after having dressed myself in the morning. Now, I saw that the most important thing I had to do was to give myself to the reading of the Word of God, and to meditation on it, that thus my heart might be comforted, encouraged, warned, reproved, instructed; and that thus, by means of the Word of God, while meditating on it, my heart might be brought into experiential communion with the Lord.

I began therefore to meditate on the New Testament from the beginning, early in the morning. The first thing I did, after having asked in a few words the Lord's blessing upon his precious Word, was, to begin to meditate on the Word of God, searching as it were into every verse, to get blessing out of it; not for the sake of the public ministry of the Word, not for the sake of preaching on what I had meditated upon, but for the sake of obtaining food for my own soul.

The result I have found to be almost invariably this, that after a very few minutes my soul has been led to confession, or to thanksgiving, or to intercession, or to supplication; so that, though I did not, as it were, give myself to prayer, but to meditation, yet it turned almost immediately more or less into prayer. When thus I have been for a while making confession or intercession, or supplication, or have given thanks, I go to the next words or verse, turning all, as I go on, into prayer for myself or others, as the Word may lead to it, but still continually keeping before me that food for my own soul is the object of my meditation. The result of this is, that there is always a good deal of confession, thanksgiving, supplication, or intercession mingled with my meditation, and then my inner man almost invariably is even sensibly nourished and strengthened, and that by breakfast time, with rare exceptions, I am in a peaceful if not happy state of heart. Thus also the Lord is pleased to communicate unto me that which, either very soon after or at a later time, I have found to become food for other believers, though it was not for the sake of the public ministry of the Word that I gave myself to meditation, but for the profit of my own inner man.

The difference, then, between my former practice and my present one is this:

Formerly, when I rose, I began to pray as soon as possible, and generally spent all my time till breakfast in prayer, or almost all the time. At all events I almost invariably began with prayer, except when I felt my soul to be more than usually barren, in which case I read the Word of God for food, or for refreshment, or for a revival and renewal of my inner man, before I gave myself to prayer.

But what was the result? I often spent a quarter of an hour, or half an hour, or even an hour, on my knees, before being conscious to myself of having derived comfort, encouragement, humbling of soul, etc., and often, after having suffered much from wandering of mind for the first ten minutes, or a quarter of an hour, or even half an hour, I only then began really to pray. I scarcely ever suffer now in this way. For my heart, first being nourished by the truth, being brought into experiential fellowship with God, I then speak to my Father and to my Friend, (vile though I am, and unworthy of it), about the things that He has brought before me in His precious Word.

It often now astonishes me that I did not sooner see this point. In no book did I ever read about it. No public ministry ever brought the matter before me. No private intercourse with a brother stirred me up to this matter. And yet, now, since God has taught me this point, it is as plain to me as anything, that the first thing the child of God has to do morning by morning is, to obtain food for his inner man. As the outward man is not fit for work for any length of time except we take food, and as this is one of the first things we do in the morning, so it should be with the inner man. We should take food for that, as every one must allow.

Now, what is the food for the inner man? Not prayer, but the Word of God; and here again, not the simple reading of the Word of God, so that it only passes through our minds, just as water runs through a pipe, but considering what we read, pondering over it, and applying it to our hearts. When we pray, we speak to God. Now, prayer, in order to be continued for any length of time in any other than a formal manner, requires, generally speaking, a measure of strength or godly desire, and the season, therefore, when this exercise of the soul can be most effectually performed is after the inner man has been nourished by meditation on the Word of God, where we find our Father speaking to us, to encourage us, to comfort us, to instruct us, to humble us, to reprove us. We may therefore profitably meditate, with God's blessing, though we are ever so weak spiritually; nay, the weaker we are, the more we need meditation for the strengthening of our inner man.

Thus there is far less to be feared from wandering of mind than if we give ourselves to prayer without having had time previously for meditation. I dwell so particularly on this point because of the immense spiritual profit and refreshment I am conscious of having derived from it myself, and I affectionately and solemnly beseech all my fellow believers to ponder this matter. By the blessing of God, I ascribe to this mode the help and strength which I have had from God to pass in peace through deeper trials, in various ways, than I had ever had before; and after having now above fourteen years tried this way, I can most fully, in the fear of God, commend it.

In addition to this I generally read, after family prayer, larger portions of the Word of God, when I still pursue my practice of reading regularly onward in the Holy Scriptures, sometimes in the New Testament, and sometimes in the Old, and for more than twenty-six years I have proved the blessedness of it. I take, also, either then or at other parts of the day, time more especially for prayer. How different, when the soul is refreshed and made happy early in the morning, from what it is when without spiritual preparation, the service, the trials, and the temptations of the day come upon one.

Notes

Chapter 1

1. George Barna, "Barna by Topic, Goals and Priorities," survey conducted in 2000, The Barna Group, http://www.barna.org/FlexPage.aspx?Page=Topic&TopicID=23.

2. George Barna, "Barna by Topic, The Bible," survey conducted in 1997, The Barna Group, http://www.barna.org/FlexPage.aspx?Page=Topic&TopicID=7.

3. *Discipleship Journal*, issue 52, page 10, http://www.navpress.com/EPubs/DisplayArticle/1/1.52.13.html.

4. Horatius Bonar, *Words Old and New* (Carlisle, PA: Banner of Truth Trust, 1866), 8.

5. J. Oswald Sanders, *Enjoying Intimacy with God* (Grand Rapids: Discovery House Publishers, 1980), 11.

Chapter 2

1. James Montgomery Boice, *Genesis* (Grand Rapids: Zondervan, 1982), 1:78.

2. Wayne Grudem, *Bible Doctrine* (Grand Rapids: Zondervan, 1999), 307–9.

3. John Piper, *Desiring God* (Sisters, OR: Multnomah Books, 1986), 80–81.

4. A. T. Pierson, *George Mueller of Bristol and His Witness to a Prayer-Hearing God* at http://www.whatsaiththescripture.com/Voice/George.Mueller.of.Bristol/George.Mueller.Bristol.L.html, Appendix L.

    Note: This appendix entry, "Soul Nourishment First," was written by George Mueller and was dated May 9, 1841. It does not appear in the print edition of the same title published by Fleming Revell, Old Tappan, NJ in 1899.

5. Ibid.

6. Ibid.

7. Ibid.

8. Sanders, *Enjoying Intimacy with God*, 90.

9. Jonathan Edwards, *Religious Affections* (Portland, OR: Multnomah Press, 1984), 3–15.

10. Ibid., 109.

11. Piper, *Desiring God*, 76.

12. Ibid., 89.

Chapter 3

1. Bonar, *Words Old and New*, 8.

2. Sanders, *Enjoying Intimacy with God*, 117.

3. Jim Berg, *Changed into His Image* (Greenville, SC: BJU Press, 1999), 115.

4. J. I. Packer, *Knowing God* (Downers Grove, IL: InterVarsity Press, 1993), 23–6.

5. Berg, *Changed into His Image*, 123.

6. George Barna. "Barna by Topic, Self Descriptions," survey conducted in 2001, The Barna Group, http://www.barna.org/FlexPage.aspx?Page=Topic&TopicID=3x.

7. Bonar, *Words Old and New*, 165.

8. Michael Horton, *The Agony of Deceit* (Chicago: Moody Press, 1990), 49.

9. Piper, *Desiring God*, 87.

10. Arthur Bennett, ed., *The Valley of Vision* (Carlisle, PA: Banner of Truth Trust, 1975), 302–3.

11. Jonathan Edwards, *The Works of Jonathan Edwards* (Boston: Doctrinal Tract and Book Society, 1850), 2:12–17.

12. "Princeton Religious Research Center, 100 Questions and Answers: Religion in America," *USA Today*, February 1, 1990.

13. *Discipleship Journal*, 10.

14. Mark Minnick, "Devotional Bible Study," audiotapes of sermons delivered at Mount Calvary Baptist Church, Greenville, SC (Greenville, SC: Taking the Word to the World).

15. Darlene Diebler Rose, http://www.heronco.com/clients/darlenerose/.

16. Don Whitney, *Spiritual Disciplines for the Christian Life*. (Colorado Springs: NavPress, 1991), 62.

17. Roger Steer, *George Müller: Delighted in God!* (Wheaton, IL: Harold Shaw, 1975), 310.

18. George Müller, *The Autobiography of George Müller* (Springdale, PA: Whitaker House, 1984), 150–51.

19. John F. MacArthur Jr., *Keys to Spiritual Growth* (Old Tappan, NJ: Fleming H. Revell, 1976), 105.

20. William Barclay, *The Gospel of Matthew* (Philadelphia: Westminster, 1958), 1:284.

21. Sanders, *Enjoying Intimacy with God*, 11.

22. Iain H. Murray, *Jonathan Edwards: A New Biography* (Carlisle, PA: Banner of Truth, 1987), 92.

23. Hank Hannegraf, *The Prayer of Jesus* (Nashville: Word Publishing, 2001), 93.

Chapter 4

1. Nathaniel Ranew, *Solitude Improved by Divine Meditation* (Morgan, PA: Soli Deo Gloria Publications, 1995), 73.

2. MacArthur, *The Keys to Spiritual Growth*, 142.

3. Ranew, *Solitude Improved by Divine Meditation*, 230–31.

4. Ibid., 66.

5. Sanders, *Enjoying Intimacy with God*, 19.

6. P. J. Achtemeier, *Harper's Bible Dictionary*, first ed. (San Francisco: Harper & Row, 1985), 1143.

7. Piper, *Desiring God*, 87.

8. Ronald Blythe, *The Pleasure of Diaries: Four Centuries of Private Writing* (New York: Pantheon, 1989), 323.

9. George Barna, "Barna by Topic, Self Descriptions," survey conducted in 2001, The Barna Group, http://www.barna.org/FlexPage.aspx?Page=Topic&TopicID=34.

10. Berg, *Changed into His Image*, 152.

11. Minnick, "Devotional Bible Study."

12. Berg, *Changed into His Image*, 173.

13. Leland Ryken, James C. Wilhoit, and Tremper Longman III, *Dictionary of Biblical Imagery* (Downers Grove, IL: InterVarsity Press, 1998), 651–54.

14. R. Kent Hughes, *Set Apart: Calling a Worldly Church to a Godly Life* (Wheaton, IL: Crossway Books), 44–5.

15. Jean Fleming, *Feeding Your Soul* (Colorado Springs: NavPress, 1999), 70.

16. "Scary Debt Stats," http://www.fool.com/ccc/secrets/secrets.htm.

17. Randy Alcorn, *Money, Possessions and Eternity* (Wheaton, IL: Tyndale, 1989), 399–400.

18. C. S. Lewis, *Mere Christianity* (New York: Macmillan, 1952), 180.

19. Mark Water, *The New Encyclopedia of Christian Quotations* (Grand Rapids, MI: Baker Books, 2000), 1061.

20. Sanders, *Enjoying Intimacy With God*, 88.

21. Water, *The New Encyclopedia of Christian Quotations*, 328.

Chapter 5

1. Barna, "Barna by topic, The Bible (1997)," May 1, 2004 (specific data no longer posted).

2. Dale Tedder, "Shepherding Hearts," http://www.southsidemethodist.org/templates/cla19gr/details.asp?id=26041&PID=285523&mast=

3. Clarence H. Faust and Thomas H. Johnson, eds., *Jonathan Edwards* (New York: Hill and Wang, 1962), 61.

4. Sanders, *Enjoying Intimacy With God*, 94.

5. Sanders, *Enjoying Intimacy With God*, 97.

6. Andrew Murray, *Humility* (Springdale, PA: Whitaker House, 1982), 12.

7. Berg, *Changed into His Image*, 26.

8. Hannegraf, *The Prayer of Jesus*, 24.

9. Sanders, *Enjoying Intimacy With God*, 40.

10. Sanders, *Enjoying Intimacy With God*, 56.

11. Sanders, *Enjoying Intimacy With God*, 53.

12. A. W. Tozer, *The Knowledge of the Holy* (San Francisco: Harper and Row, 1961), 1–2.

13. Steve Pettit, *How to Pray Thirty Minutes a Day* (Pembine, WI: Heart Publications, 1996), 10-11.

14. Piper, *Desiring God*, 138.

15. Piper, *Desiring God*, 139.

16. Hannegraf, *The Prayer of Jesus*, 10.

17. Pettit, *How to Pray Thirty Minutes a Day*, 21.

Chapter 6

1. James Strong, *Enhanced Strong's Lexicon*, electronic ed. (Bellingham, WA: Logos Research Systems, 1995)

2. Edythe Draper, *Draper's Book of Quotations for the Christian World*. (Wheaton, IL: Tyndale House Publishers, 1992), 225.

3. Gary Inrig, *Quality Friendship: The Risks and Rewards* (Chicago: Moody Press, 1981), 55.

4. Ibid., 173.

5. W. E. Vine, *Vine's Complete Expository Dictionary of Old and New Testament Words* (Nashville: Thomas Nelson Publishers, 1966), 50.

6. Craig Brian Larson and Leadership Journal, *750 Engaging Illustrations for Preachers, Teachers, and Writers*, (Grand Rapids, MI: Baker Book House, 1993), 421.

7. Inrig, *Quality Friendship: The Risks and Rewards*, 79.

8. Charles R. Swindoll, *Swindoll's Ultimate Book of Illustrations and Quotes* (Nashville: Thomas Nelson Publishers, 1998), 222.

9. Strong, *Enhanced Strong's Lexicon*, electronic ed.

10. Elisabeth Elliot, *Shadow of the Almighty* (San Francisco: Harper & Collins, 1958), 43.

Chapter 7

1. C. Matthew McMahon, "The Eschatological Mastery of the World & Meditation," http://www.apuritansmind.com/ChristianWalk/ McMahonEschatologicalMasteryMeditation.htm.

2. James Strong, *The Exhaustive Concordance of the Bible*, electronic ed. (Ontario: Woodside Bible Fellowship, 1996).

3. R. Laird Harris, Gleason L. Archer, G. L., and Bruce K. Waltke, *Theological Wordbook of the Old Testament*, electronic ed. (Chicago: Moody Press, 1999)

4. Strong, *The Exhaustive Concordance of the Bible*, electronic ed.

5. Harris, *Theological Wordbook of the Old Testament*, electronic ed.

6. Packer, *Knowing God*, 18–19.

7. Merrill F. Unger, *Unger's Bible Dictionary* (Chicago: Moody Press, 1957), 709.

8. Minnick, "*Devotional Bible Reading.*"

9. Ranew, *Solitude Improved by Divine Meditation*, 231.

10. W. E. Vine, *Expository Dictionary of New Testament Words* (Old Tappan, NJ: Fleming Revell, 1966), 345.

11. Minnick, "*Devotional Bible Reading.*"

12. Jim Berg, *Created for His Glory*, (Greenville, SC: BJU Press, 2002) 8–13.

13. Vine, *Expository Dictionary of New Testament Words*, 153.

14. Ranew, *Solitude Improved by Divine Meditation*, 60.

15. Ibid., 58.

16. Andrew Murray, *Like Christ* (Springdale, PA: Whitaker House, 1983), 148.

17. A.W. Tozer, *Knowledge of the Holy* (San Francisco, CA: Harper, 1978), 82.

18. "Meditation on God" sermon by Charles Haddon Spurgeon delivered Summer, 1858. Sermon printed at www.biblebb.com/files/ spurgeon/2690.HTM.

19. Ranew, *Solitude Improved by Divine Meditation*, 98.

20. Ibid., 9.

21. Ibid., 29.

22. Ibid., p. 34.

23. Ibid., 89–90.

24. Ibid., 3.

Chapter 8

1. John G. Paton, *John G. Paton: Missionary to the New Hebrides* (Carlisle, PA: Banner of Truth, 1994), 14.

2. Ibid., 15.

3. Ibid., 16.

4. Ibid., 8.

5. Ibid., 14–5.

6. Ibid., 21.

7. Ibid., 56.

Appendix

1. Pierson, *George Mueller of Bristol and His Witness to a Prayer-Hearing God*, Appendix L.

Alone with **God**